PROLOGUE

This book is not about the recent events that are briefly described below. It is about our history and the legacy of The Slave Patrol's impact on modern day Law Enforcement. A legacy that allows black people to be treated as less than human.

A white neighbor (Karen) phoned a County Deputy and complained that two Black men were staying with a white woman inside a Mississippi home. That Deputy told another Deputy who texted a group of white officers (The Slave Patrol) so willing to use excessive force they called themselves "The Goon Squad."
The six officers entered a house without a warrant and handcuffed and assaulted the two black men with stun guns, a sex toy and other objects. The officers mocked them with racial slurs and made them shower together to remove evidence, all during a 90-minute torture session, they then devised a cover-up that included planting drugs and a gun, leading to false charges that stood against the victims for months.
An officer forced one of the victims to his knees for a "mock execution," intending to fire the gun without a bullet. But it was loaded, and discharged, cutting his tongue, breaking his jaw and exiting through his neck.
The brutality visited upon these victims was not a botched police operation, nor was it an isolated incident. This is happening on a spectrum everyday, all under the authority of a badge. All six officers charged have pleaded gulity and are awaiting sentencing.

Investigating the roots of societal structures and historical legacies leads to a profound understanding of the entrenched nature of systemic racism and oppression. Systemic racism and oppression refer to the institutional patterns and practices that systematically disadvantage certain groups based on race or ethnicity. These systems are deeply ingrained in various aspects of society, including education, healthcare, employment, and criminal justice.

It's all "Hidden In Plain Sight", we just need to pay attention.

TABLE OF CONTENTS
Chapter 1: Introduction

Definition and Purpose of Slave Patrols

Significance of Studying Slave Patrols in Understanding Systemic Racism

Chapter 2: Origins of Slave Patrols Early Forms of Slave Control in Colonial America

Emergence of Formalized Slave Patrols in Southern Colonies

Legal Foundations and Mandates for Slave Patrols

Chapter 3: Functions and Operations of Slave Patrols

Roles and Responsibilities of Slave Patrol Members

Tactics and Methods Employed by Slave Patrols

Relationship between Slave Patrols and Plantation Owners

Slave Patrols and the Expansion of the Plantation Economy in the Antebellum South

Chapter 4: Resistance and Rebellion against Slave Patrols

Slave Strategies for Evading Capture and Surveillance by Slave Patrols

Instances of Armed Resistance against Slave Patrols

Influence of Slave Resistance on Slave Patrol Tactics and Policies

Chapter 5: Evolution of Slave Patrols Post-Emancipation

Transition of Slave Patrols to Law Enforcement Agencies

Continuation of Racially Biased Policing Practices after Slave Patrols

Legacy of Slave Patrols in Modern Law Enforcement

Chapter 6: Case Studies and Examples

Specific Instances of Slave Patrol Operations and Their Impacts

Examination of Notable Legal Cases Involving Slave Patrols

Comparative Analysis across Different Regions and Time Periods

Chapter 7: Cultural and Societal Impact of Slave Patrols

Slave Patrols Influence on Racial Attitudes and Stereotypes

Slave Patrols Perpetuation of Inequality and Social Hierarchies

Cultural Memory and Representation of Slave Patrols in Art and Literature

Chapter 8: Legacy and Reckoning

Repercussions of Slave Patrols on Contemporary Society

Calls for Acknowledgment, Reparation, and Reconciliation Due to Slave Patrols

Steps toward Addressing Systemic Racism Rooted in Slave Patrols

Chapter 9: Conclusion

Reflection on the Enduring Impact of Slave Patrols

CHAPTER 1: INTRODUCTION

Definition and Purpose of Slave Patrols

Slave patrols in the 18th century Southern United States were created to enforce slavery and control **enslaved individuals** for the benefit of slaveholders economically. These patrols, backed by laws like the **Fugitive Slave Acts**, upheld **white supremacy** and subjugated Black people. Organized by white landowners, their duties included rule enforcement, preventing rebellion, and using force to maintain the status quo. The relationship with enslaved individuals was marked by fear and brutality, leaving a lasting impact on societal structures. The modern-day targeting and violence against African Americans by law enforcement echoes the historical oppression by **slave patrols**, highlighting ongoing **systemic racism**.

Key Takeaways

- Slave patrols enforced slavery in the Southern US.
- They controlled and surveilled enslaved populations.
- Supported by legal acts like the Fugitive Slave Acts.
- Rooted in white supremacy and subjugation of Black people.
- Tied to the economic interests of slaveholders.

Historical Context of Slave Patrols

In exploring the historical context of **slave patrols**, it is important to thoroughly investigate the **societal structures** and power dynamics that shaped the origins and evolution of these vigilante groups. Slave patrols emerged in the **Southern United States** during the **18th century** as a means of enforcing the institution of slavery and maintaining control over the enslaved population. The establishment of these patrols was deeply intertwined with the **economic interests** of slaveholders, who relied on the forced labor of enslaved individuals for their agricultural enterprises.

Additionally, the **legal framework** of the time, including the **Fugitive Slave Acts**, provided slave patrols with the authority to apprehend and punish enslaved individuals attempting to escape bondage. The **racial hierarchy** of the antebellum South further fueled the formation of these patrols, as they operated on the premise of white supremacy and the subjugation of Black people.

Understanding the historical context of slave patrols is essential for comprehending their lasting impact on American society and the **systemic racism** that persists today. By delving into the roots of these vigilante groups, we can gain insights into the complex dynamics that perpetuated slavery and oppression.

Formation and Structure of Patrols

The organization and hierarchy of **slave patrols** were meticulously designed to assert control over enslaved individuals and maintain order within the slaveholding society of the Southern United States. These patrols typically consisted of white men, often **wealthy landowners** or planters, who were appointed as patrollers to oversee the enslaved population. The structure of these patrols varied across different regions but generally followed a **hierarchical system** where a captain or **patrol leader** was in charge, overseeing a group of patrollers who would conduct regular rounds to monitor the movements and behaviors of enslaved individuals.

In some areas, slave patrols were organized at the county level, with each patrol assigned to specific geographic areas. Patrollers were granted **broad authority** to stop, search, and interrogate enslaved individuals, often supported by **local laws** that upheld their actions. The hierarchical structure of slave patrols not only facilitated surveillance and control but also served as a means of **social control**, reinforcing the power dynamics of the slaveholding society.

Duties and Responsibilities of Patrollers

Patrollers in the system of **slave patrols** were tasked with **enforcing the rules** and regulations imposed upon enslaved individuals within the Southern United States. These patrollers were responsible for **maintaining control and order** on plantations, preventing any attempts at rebellion or escape by enslaved individuals. Their duties included **conducting regular patrols** of the area, monitoring the movements of enslaved individuals, and ensuring that they were not engaging in any activities deemed threatening to the institution of slavery.

Additionally, patrollers were expected to apprehend any enslaved individuals found without proper authorization or outside of their designated work areas. They were also responsible for **investigating any reports of misconduct** or disobedience among the enslaved population. Patrollers had the authority to **use physical force**, including violence, to maintain discipline and uphold the hierarchical structure of slavery. Their presence **instilled fear** among the enslaved community, serving as a constant reminder of their subordinate status and the consequences of resistance. The duties and responsibilities of patrollers were integral to the functioning of the **oppressive system of slavery** in the antebellum South.

Relationship with Enslaved Individuals

With their role deeply embedded in the **enforcement of slavery**, the interaction between patrollers and enslaved individuals was characterized by a **power dynamic** that perpetuated fear and control. Patrollers held significant authority over the enslaved population, using tactics such as **brutal punishments**, surveillance, and intimidation to maintain order and compliance.

Enslaved individuals lived under **constant surveillance** and endured **harsh treatment** at the hands of these patrollers. The relationship was marked by fear, as any resistance or attempt to escape would result in severe consequences, including physical punishment or even death. Enslaved individuals were stripped of their autonomy and subjected to **dehumanizing treatment**, reinforcing the oppressive system of slavery.

The power dynamics inherent in the relationship between patrollers and enslaved individuals underscore the brutal reality of the institution of slavery, highlighting the pervasive control exerted by those in **positions of authority**.

Impact on African American Communities

Indisputably intertwined with the fabric of African American communities, the **legacy of slave patrols** reverberates through generations, leaving a **lasting imprint on societal structures** and collective memory. The historical presence of slave patrols instilled fear and a **sense of constant surveillance** among African Americans, shaping their interactions with law enforcement and authority figures for years to come. This pervasive fear led to the development of **coping**

mechanisms and survival strategies within these communities, influencing behaviors and attitudes towards law enforcement.

Furthermore, the establishment of slave patrols reinforced white supremacy and **perpetuated racial hierarchies**, creating **deep-rooted inequalities** that continue to impact African American communities today. The systematic oppression and violence inflicted by slave patrols have contributed to the **enduring mistrust of law enforcement** among African Americans and the ongoing struggle for racial justice and equality. The legacy of slave patrols serves as a stark reminder of the historical injustices faced by African Americans and underscores the importance of addressing **systemic racism in contemporary society**.

Resistance and Abolition Movements

The enduring legacy of **slave patrols** in African American communities paved the way for robust **resistance** and **abolition movements** aimed at challenging the oppressive system of surveillance and control.

In response to the constant threat and violence imposed by slave patrols, African Americans organized various forms of resistance. This included acts of sabotage, escape attempts, and the establishment of secret networks like the **Underground Railroad** to help enslaved individuals find freedom.

Abolition movements, led by both African Americans and white allies, gained momentum in the fight against the institution of slavery. Figures like **Harriet Tubman**, **Frederick Douglass**, and Sojourner Truth became prominent voices advocating for the abolition of slavery and the recognition of the humanity and rights of African Americans.

These movements were instrumental in raising awareness about the atrocities of slavery and ultimately contributed to its abolition in the United States through events like the Civil War and the **Emancipation Proclamation**.

Legacy and Repercussions Today

What enduring societal impacts do the historical slave patrols continue to have on African American communities today?

The legacy of slave patrols persists in various ways, shaping the experiences of African Americans in contemporary society. The **systemic oppression** and **dehumanization** enforced by slave patrols have contributed to the **deep-rooted racism** and prejudice that continue to plague African American communities. The distrust between African Americans and law enforcement can be traced back to the origins of slave patrols, perpetuating tensions and impacting interactions between the two groups.

Furthermore, the **disproportionate targeting and violence** towards African Americans by law enforcement can be seen as a modern-day manifestation of the **control and surveillance tactics** employed by slave patrols. The ongoing struggle for justice and equality in the face of **institutionalized discrimination** reflects the enduring impact of historical slave patrols on African American communities.

Addressing these deep-seated issues requires a thorough understanding of their historical context and a commitment to dismantling **systems of oppression** that continue to perpetuate inequality and injustice.

Conclusion

To sum up, **slave patrols** operated as a pervasive and oppressive force in American history, akin to the shadows that loomed over the lives of enslaved individuals. Their formation, duties, and impact on African American communities were deeply rooted in maintaining control and perpetuating **systems of oppression**.

Despite resistance and abolition movements, the legacy of slave patrols continues to reverberate through society today, casting a long shadow over the **collective memory** of the nation.

Significance of Studying Slave Patrols in Understanding Systemic Racism

Studying **slave patrols** reveals their deep influence on **systemic racism** in the U.S. These patrols, born in the colonial era, enforced control through fear and violence. Their legacy impacts modern policing, perpetuating **racial biases** and disparities. Understanding their origins is essential for tackling entrenched inequities. Their role in maintaining **white supremacy** and oppressing Black communities continues to shape social, economic, and legal structures today. By exploring these origins, one uncovers how racism and discrimination have been ingrained into society. Discovering the **lasting effects** of slave patrols is important for grasping the complexities of systemic racism in America.

Key Takeaways

- Understanding slave patrols reveals the roots of modern policing and its connection to systemic racism.
- Studying slave patrols helps uncover the historical foundation of racial biases in law enforcement.
- Slave patrols' impact on Black communities highlights enduring disparities and mistrust in authority.
- Examining slave patrols sheds light on how oppression and control shaped structures of power.
- Analyzing slave patrols is crucial for addressing systemic racism and promoting equity in society.

Role in Enforcing Racial Control

Playing a pivotal role in shaping racial dynamics and reinforcing systems of control, **slave patrols** in the United States were instrumental in **perpetuating systemic racism** through their enforcement mechanisms. These patrols, consisting of armed white men tasked with monitoring and controlling the movements of enslaved individuals, operated under the guise of **maintaining order** and protecting property.

However, their true function was to assert dominance over Black individuals, instill fear, and uphold the **racial hierarchy** of the time. By actively surveilling and policing the activities of enslaved people, slave patrols not only restricted their physical freedom but also sought to suppress any potential **acts of resistance** or rebellion.

Furthermore, slave patrols were granted broad authority to use **violence and intimidation tactics**, often with impunity, to maintain control over enslaved populations. This **unchecked power** not only perpetuated the dehumanization of Black individuals but also normalized violence as a means of **racial subjugation**.

Understanding the role of slave patrols in enforcing racial control is pivotal in comprehending the deep-rooted nature of systemic racism in the United States.

Impact on Black Communities

Demonstrating a lasting legacy of oppression and trauma, the impact of **slave patrols** on **Black communities** reverberates through generations, shaping **societal structures** and perpetuating **systemic inequities**. The presence of slave patrols instilled fear and control within Black communities, leading to a **deep-seated mistrust** of law enforcement and authority figures that continues to persist today. The trauma inflicted by these patrols, which often involved violence, surveillance, and dehumanization, has had profound **psychological effects** on Black individuals and communities, contributing to feelings of marginalization and insecurity.

Moreover, the historical role of slave patrols in maintaining **white supremacy** has had far-reaching consequences on the **economic and social conditions** of Black communities. The systematic oppression and exploitation of Black individuals through slavery and its enforcement mechanisms, such as slave patrols, have created enduring disparities in wealth, education, and access to opportunities. These disparities continue to shape the lived experiences of Black Americans, perpetuating cycles of poverty and limited mobility.

Understanding the impact of slave patrols on Black communities is essential in recognizing the deep-rooted origins of **systemic racism** and working towards meaningful societal change.

Connection to Modern Policing

Drawing a parallel between the historical practices of **slave patrols** and contemporary law enforcement reveals a continuum of **systemic racism** embedded within the structure and operations of **modern policing**. The origins of modern policing in the United States can be traced back to the slave patrols that were tasked with controlling and subjugating enslaved populations. These patrols, formed to protect the economic interests of slave owners and maintain social order, laid the foundation for the development of **law enforcement agencies**. The hierarchical and authoritarian nature of slave patrols can still be seen in many police departments today, where power differentials and **racial biases** persist.

Furthermore, the tactics employed by slave patrols, such as **surveillance**, intimidation, and violence, have carried over into modern policing practices. This continuity underscores how **historical systems of oppression** have shaped the current landscape of law enforcement, perpetuating racial disparities and injustices. Understanding this connection is vital for addressing systemic racism within police institutions and working towards **meaningful reform** that prioritizes equity and justice for all communities.

Perpetuation of Racial Biases

An examination of **contemporary law enforcement practices** reveals a persistent perpetuation of **racial biases** rooted in **historical systems of oppression**. Despite advancements and changes in society, racial biases continue to influence interactions between law enforcement and **minority communities**. Studies have shown that individuals from racial and ethnic minority groups are **disproportionately targeted**, stopped, and subjected to the **use of force** by law enforcement compared to their white counterparts. This perpetuation of bias is evident in various aspects of policing, including traffic stops, arrests, and the treatment of individuals in custody.

Implicit biases held by individuals within law enforcement, shaped by **societal stereotypes** and prejudices, further exacerbate the issue. These biases can influence split-second decisions made by officers during encounters with civilians, leading to **discriminatory outcomes**. Additionally, the historical role of **slave patrols** in enforcing racial control and subjugation has left a lasting impact on the structure and practices of modern law enforcement agencies, contributing to the perpetuation of racial biases in policing.

Addressing and dismantling these biases is important in working towards a more equitable and just criminal justice system.

Influence on Legal System

The historical legacy of **slave patrols** continues to exert a significant influence on the structure and operations of the **legal system** in the United States, shaping its approach to policing and criminal justice. The origins of **modern policing** in the U.S. can be traced back to these patrols, which were tasked with controlling and subjugating enslaved populations. This early form of policing was deeply intertwined with **racial oppression** and the maintenance of the institution of slavery. As a result, the legal system today continues to grapple with issues of **racial bias**, discrimination, and unequal treatment, reflecting the systemic nature of racism that has persisted over generations.

The influence of slave patrols on the legal system is evident in various aspects, including the over-policing of Black communities, racial profiling, harsher sentencing for people of color, and racial disparities in the **criminal justice system**. These issues highlight the enduring impact of **historical practices** on contemporary law enforcement and underscore the urgent need for reform to address **systemic racism** within the legal system.

Legacy of Oppression

Evidenced through **patterns of institutional discrimination** and societal inequalities, the **enduring legacy of oppression** stemming from slave patrols continues to permeate various facets of contemporary American society. The historical roots of slave patrols, which were designed to control and oppress enslaved individuals, have left a lasting impact on the social, economic, and political structures of the United States. This legacy of oppression is evident in the **disparities seen in areas** such as wealth accumulation, educational attainment, and access to healthcare among different racial groups.

The **systemic inequalities** that originated from slave patrols have contributed to the marginalization and disenfranchisement of Black communities, **perpetuating cycles of poverty** and limited opportunities for advancement. The **deep-seated prejudices and biases** embedded in American society as a result of this **oppressive history** continue to influence interactions between individuals of different races and shape institutional practices.

Understanding the legacy of oppression left by slave patrols is essential in addressing current **social injustices** and working towards a more equitable and inclusive society. By recognizing and confronting these historical injustices, steps can be taken to **dismantle systemic racism** and aim towards a future where all individuals are treated with fairness and dignity.

Implications for Social Justice

Rooted in the **enduring legacy** of oppression left by slave patrols, the implications for **social justice** highlight the **systemic challenges** that persist in **contemporary American society**. The historical foundation of slave patrols, which were instrumental in enforcing and maintaining the institution of slavery, has shaped the **structures of power** and privilege that continue to disadvantage **marginalized communities** today. Understanding the role of slave patrols allows for a critical examination of how racism, discrimination, and inequality are deeply ingrained in the fabric of society.

Examining the implications for social justice in the context of slave patrols reveals the ongoing struggle for equality and equity. By recognizing the historical roots of **systemic racism**, society can begin to address the pivotal issues that perpetuate injustices. This understanding is vital for implementing effective policies, interventions, and initiatives aimed at dismantling **oppressive**

systems and advancing social justice. It underscores the importance of promoting fairness, inclusivity, and respect for all individuals, regardless of race, ethnicity, or background. Ultimately, acknowledging the implications of slave patrols on social justice is essential for creating a more just and **equitable society** for future generations.

Conclusion

To summarize, the examination of **slave patrols** is essential in understanding **systemic racism**. One **striking statistic** is that in some southern states, slave patrols outnumbered the actual slave population by a ratio of 3 to 1. This disparity highlights the extent to which these patrols were used to maintain control and suppress Black communities.

By scrutinizing the historical origins and lasting impact of slave patrols, we can better comprehend the **ongoing legacy** of oppression and work towards achieving social justice.

CHAPTER 2: ORIGINS OF SLAVE PATROLS

Early Forms of Slave Control in Colonial America

Early forms of slave control in Colonial America involved **harsh physical punishments** like whippings and branding, **restrictive measures** such as curfews and leg irons, and **surveillance techniques** through overseers and informants. Enslaved individuals faced **rigorous labor regulations**, punitive actions for disobedience, and psychological manipulation. Legal codes reinforced subordinate status and limited autonomy, while community surveillance maintained compliance. **Resistance took forms** of defiance, rebellions, and cultural preservation. This systematic control and resistance dynamic shaped the complex landscape of slavery in Colonial America, highlighting the relentless struggle for power and autonomy.

Key Takeaways

- Physical punishment like whippings, branding, and confinement in stocks were common.
- Restrictive measures included curfews, prohibition of property ownership, and use of leg irons.
- Surveillance techniques like overseers, informants, and random inspections were employed.
- Work regulations involved rigorous schedules, long hours, and constant threat of punishment.
- Punitive actions for disobedience included whipping, being sold, and public humiliation.

Physical Punishment Methods

Various **physical punishment methods** were employed in colonial America as a means of controlling slaves. Whippings were a common form of discipline, with slaves often subjected to **brutal lashings** for disobedience or attempting to escape. The severity of the whipping varied, ranging from a few lashes to hundreds, depending on the offense committed. In addition to whippings, slaves could also face other forms of physical punishment such as branding, mutilation, or even **public humiliation**.

One particularly cruel method of punishment was known as **'lashing at the stake,'** where a slave would be tied to a stake and whipped in front of their fellow slaves as a deterrent against rebellion. This public display of violence served to instill fear and reinforce the **power dynamics of slavery**. Other physical punishments included **confinement in stocks** or irons, where slaves would be immobilized for a period as a form of punishment or public spectacle.

Restrictive Measures and Devices

In addition to **physical punishment methods**, colonial America also employed a range of **restrictive measures** and devices to control and constrain the movements and freedoms of slaves. These measures were designed to limit the autonomy of slaves and prevent any attempts at rebellion or escape. One common restrictive measure was the implementation of **curfews**, where slaves were required to be indoors by a certain time each evening, restricting their movement during nighttime hours. Additionally, slaves were often prohibited from **owning property**, carrying weapons, or gathering in groups without supervision.

Restrictive devices were also utilized to physically constrain slaves. **Leg irons**, shackles, and chains were commonly used to limit the mobility of slaves, making it harder for them to escape or resist their owners. **Collars with bells** attached were sometimes used to track the movements of slaves, especially those working in remote areas. These measures not only restricted the physical movements of slaves but also served as a constant reminder of their **subservient status** and **lack of freedom** in colonial America.

Surveillance and Monitoring Techniques

Utilizing a network of **overseers** and **informants**, colonial authorities implemented intricate **surveillance** and **monitoring** techniques to closely observe the activities and interactions of slaves in order to maintain control and **prevent uprisings**. Overseers were tasked with supervising the daily tasks of slaves on plantations, ensuring compliance with rules, and reporting any signs of disobedience. These overseers often used **intimidation** and violence to assert their authority and keep slaves in line.

In addition to overseers, informants played a vital role in surveillance efforts. These informants were fellow slaves who were coerced or incentivized to report on the activities of their peers. This system created a pervasive atmosphere of distrust and fear among the slave community, making it challenging for any organized **resistance** to take shape without being discovered.

Furthermore, colonial authorities employed tactics such as random inspections, curfews, and pass systems to monitor and restrict the movements of slaves. These surveillance and monitoring techniques were essential tools in maintaining the **oppressive** system of slavery in colonial America.

Work and Labor Regulations

The implementation of strict **work and labor regulations** in colonial America played a pivotal role in maintaining control over enslaved individuals and maximizing productivity within the oppressive system of slavery. Enslaved individuals were subjected to **rigorous schedules and tasks** that were often **physically demanding and repetitive**. They were expected to **work from sunrise to sunset**, with minimal rest periods, and any deviation from these rules resulted in severe consequences.

Enslaved individuals were assigned specific roles based on their perceived physical abilities and skills, with little to no consideration for their personal interests or well-being. This **division of labor** was crafted to guarantee the **efficient operation of plantations** and other industries reliant on slave labor. Additionally, enslaved individuals were often forced to work under the **constant threat of punishment**, further reinforcing the power dynamics inherent in the system of slavery.

Punitive Actions for Disobedience

Enslaved individuals in colonial America faced **punitive actions** for disobedience as a means of reinforcing control and discipline within the **oppressive system** of slavery. Punitive measures were harsh and often aimed at instilling fear and ensuring compliance. **Physical punishment**, such as **whipping**, was a common form of discipline for disobedient slaves. The severity of the whipping varied depending on the offense committed, with more serious infractions resulting in brutal beatings that left lasting physical and emotional scars on the individuals.

In addition to physical punishment, **enslaved individuals** could also face other punitive actions such as being sold away from their families, forced labor on plantations with **harsher conditions**, or even being subjected to **public humiliation** as a deterrent to others. These measures were designed to maintain order and control within the slave community, emphasizing the **power dynamics** of the oppressive system. The use of punitive actions for disobedience highlights the brutal reality of slavery in colonial America and the lengths to which slave owners would go to maintain dominance and submission.

Psychological Tactics and Manipulation

Employing **psychological tactics** and manipulation, slave owners in colonial America strategically exploited the **mental and emotional vulnerabilities** of enslaved individuals to maintain control and authority within the oppressive system of slavery. By **instilling fear**, **fostering dependency**, and **undermining self-worth**, slave owners aimed to break the spirit and resistance of their slaves. **Psychological manipulation** was a tool used to enforce obedience and discourage any notions of rebellion or escape.

Slave owners often employed tactics such as isolation, manipulation of familial bonds, and psychological conditioning to maintain dominance over their enslaved workforce. By separating families, creating rivalries among slaves, and using **rewards and punishments** to control behavior, slave owners **perpetuated a cycle** of psychological control that reinforced the power dynamics of slavery.

The psychological tactics and manipulation used by slave owners in colonial America were aimed at **dehumanizing enslaved individuals**, eroding their sense of self-worth, and ensuring compliance with the oppressive system of slavery. These tactics not only inflicted mental and emotional suffering but also served to uphold the institution of slavery by suppressing resistance and rebellion.

Control of Communication and Information

Strategically **controlling communication and information** was a key aspect of maintaining dominance and authority over enslaved individuals in colonial America. Slave owners implemented various methods to regulate the flow of information among the enslaved population. One common tactic was **restricting access to education** and literacy, as knowledge was seen as a threat to the existing power dynamics. Enslaved individuals were often prohibited from learning to read and write, limiting their ability to communicate and share information among themselves.

Furthermore, slave owners **closely monitored and censored conversations** among the enslaved population. Any form of communication that was deemed **rebellious or insubordinate** was met with **severe punishment, instilling fear** and discouraging open dialogue. Additionally, slave patrols and overseers were utilized to **eavesdrop on conversations and report** any suspicious activities back to the slave owners.

Legal Codes and Restrictions

The regulation of **enslaved individuals** in colonial America extended beyond control of communication and information to encompass a system of **legal codes** and restrictions designed to further solidify the power dynamics between slave owners and the enslaved population. These legal codes were implemented to maintain order, reinforce the **subordinate status** of enslaved individuals, and **protect the interests** of slave owners. Restrictions were imposed on various aspects of enslaved life, including movement, assembly, education, and marriage.

One of the most significant legal restrictions was the **denial of basic human rights** to the enslaved population. Enslaved individuals were considered property under the law, stripped of their autonomy and subjected to the will of their owners. Punishments for disobedience or resistance were severe, often including **physical abuse** or even death. Additionally, laws were enacted to prevent enslaved individuals from **seeking freedom** through escape or rebellion, further entrenching their subjugated status.

These legal codes and restrictions formed an integral part of the **oppressive system** of control in colonial America, perpetuating the dehumanization and exploitation of enslaved individuals for the **economic gain** of their owners.

Community and Social Surveillance

Monitoring and control of **enslaved communities** in colonial America extended beyond legal restrictions to encompass a network of community and social surveillance mechanisms. This system of surveillance was essential for maintaining order and ensuring the compliance of enslaved individuals with the established norms and expectations of the society. Enslaved people were subjected to **constant monitoring** by plantation owners, overseers, and other white individuals within the community. This surveillance often took the form of strict supervision of daily activities, **restrictions on movement**, and the **regulation of social interactions**. Enslaved individuals had **limited privacy and autonomy**, with their actions and behaviors closely scrutinized at all times.

Furthermore, enslaved communities themselves played a role in monitoring and policing their members. **Peer surveillance** was common, where enslaved individuals reported any deviant behavior or signs of resistance to the authorities. This **internal surveillance system** created a **sense of fear and mistrust** among the enslaved population, making it challenging for them to organize and resist their oppressors.

Resistance and Rebellions

Resistance and **rebellions** among enslaved individuals in colonial America were significant expressions of defiance against the **oppressive systems of control** in place. Enslaved people faced unimaginable hardships, yet many found ways to resist their subjugation. From **acts of everyday resistance** such as feigning illness or breaking tools to more overt forms of rebellion like running away or organizing uprisings, enslaved individuals continuously challenged the status quo.

One of the most well-known rebellions in colonial America was the **Stono Rebellion of 1739** in South Carolina, where a group of enslaved Africans rose up, killing several whites and attempting to escape to Spanish Florida. This event led to **stricter slave codes** and increased surveillance of enslaved populations.

Resistance was not limited to large-scale rebellions; it also manifested in subtle forms such as preserving **African cultural traditions**, creating **tight-knit communities**, and passing down **stories of resistance** to future generations. These acts of defiance were pivotal in maintaining a sense of identity and autonomy in the face of brutal oppression.

Conclusion

In examining early forms of slave control in colonial America, it is evident that a complex system of **physical punishment**, **restrictive measures**, surveillance techniques, **labor regulations**, punitive actions, communication control, legal restrictions, and social surveillance were employed to maintain control over enslaved individuals.

Despite these oppressive methods, resistance and rebellions were common as enslaved individuals fought against the dehumanizing and exploitative practices of their oppressors. The struggle for freedom and autonomy persisted, challenging the **unjust systems of control** in colonial America.

Emergence of Formalized Slave Patrols in Southern Colonies

The formalization of **slave patrols** in the Southern colonies marked a pivotal step in controlling enslaved individuals and upholding the **racial hierarchy** of slavery. Patrollers were empowered by laws to monitor and enforce order, fueling racial biases and systemic oppression. Structured at the county level, **armed patrols** oversaw movements, checked passes, and enforced curfews, instilling fear and restricting freedoms. Despite resistance, the legacy of these patrols persists in modern societal inequalities and **systemic racism**. Understanding this history offers vital insights into ongoing injustices and the need for addressing deep-rooted biases.

Key Takeaways

- Slave patrols formalized in response to fear of slave revolts.
- Emerged as a means to control and monitor enslaved population.
- Legal foundations granted broad authority to white patrols.
- Organized at the county level with appointed white patrollers.
- Equipped with weapons, patrols enforced racial hierarchy and control.

Early Forms of Slave Monitoring

In response to the pervasive fear of **slave revolts** and uprisings in the Southern colonies, early forms of **slave monitoring** began to take shape as a means of asserting control over the enslaved population. Plantation owners and overseers utilized various methods to monitor the movements and activities of slaves, aiming to prevent any potential rebellions.

One common practice was the establishment of **curfews**, where slaves were required to return to their quarters by a certain hour each evening. Additionally, **patrols** consisting of **white men** were often organized to conduct regular **inspections** of plantations, checking for any signs of unrest or resistance among the enslaved individuals.

Slave monitoring also extended to the use of **informants** within the slave community. Owners incentivized certain trusted slaves with privileges or favors in exchange for reporting on the behavior and conversations of their peers. This system not only instilled a **sense of distrust** and division among the enslaved population but also served as a method of surveillance to detect any signs of dissent or insubordination.

These early forms of monitoring laid the groundwork for the more formalized slave patrols that would later emerge in the Southern colonies.

Legal Foundations of Patrols

Amidst the growing concerns of maintaining control over the **enslaved population** in the Southern colonies, the legal foundations of **formalized slave patrols** began to take shape as a response to the perceived threats of insurrection.

As early as the 17th century, colonial legislatures passed laws that empowered **white patrols** to monitor and regulate the movements of enslaved individuals. These laws not only formalized the existence of slave patrols but also granted them **broad authority** to stop, search, and apprehend any enslaved person deemed suspicious or engaged in unauthorized activities.

The legal basis for these patrols often rested on **racialized assumptions** of Black inferiority and the necessity of control to prevent uprisings. Additionally, laws were enacted to absolve patrol members of any liability for violence or mistreatment inflicted upon enslaved individuals during patrol duties.

This **legal immunity** further entrenched the oppressive nature of slave patrols and facilitated their role as enforcers of the **racial hierarchy** within the colonies.

Structure and Organization of Patrols

During this period, the organization and structure of **slave patrols** in the Southern colonies underwent meticulous planning and implementation to guarantee effective control over the enslaved population. Slave patrols were typically organized at the **county level**, with each county appointing a group of **white men** to serve as **patrollers**. These patrols were often overseen by local officials or wealthy **plantation owners**, ensuring that the patrols had the authority and resources to carry out their duties effectively.

The structure of these patrols varied, but they commonly consisted of **small groups** of patrollers who would regularly patrol the roads, plantations, and public spaces to monitor the movements and activities of enslaved individuals. Patrollers were required to work in shifts, often during the night, to prevent potential **slave revolts** or escapes. Additionally, patrols were equipped with **weapons** such as guns, whips, and dogs to assist in apprehending and controlling enslaved individuals. This structured approach to organizing and deploying patrols contributed to maintaining order and control over the enslaved population in the Southern colonies.

Duties and Responsibilities of Patrollers

What specific duties and responsibilities were assigned to the **patrollers** within the structured slave patrol system in the Southern colonies?

Patrollers in the Southern colonies had a range of duties and responsibilities aimed at maintaining control over enslaved populations. These duties included **monitoring** the movements of enslaved individuals, checking **travel passes** to make sure enslaved individuals had permission to be off the plantation, and preventing gatherings of enslaved people without supervision.

Patrollers were also tasked with **enforcing curfews** for enslaved individuals, **inspecting living quarters** for any signs of **potential uprisings** or escape plans, and apprehending any enslaved individuals found outside of their **designated areas** without proper authorization.

Additionally, patrollers were responsible for reporting any suspicious activities or behaviors they observed among the enslaved population to plantation owners or **local authorities**. The role of patrollers was integral to the maintenance of the slave patrol system, as their presence and actions were intended to instill fear and control among the enslaved population.

Relationship with Local Authorities

The relationship between **patrollers** operating within the structured **slave patrol system** in the Southern colonies and **local authorities** was characterized by a symbiotic dynamic that reinforced the control and surveillance mechanisms over the enslaved population. Local authorities, often consisting of wealthy landowners, politicians, or influential community members, provided legal and institutional support to the slave patrols. They sanctioned the patrollers' actions, legitimizing their activities under the guise of maintaining **social order** and protecting **property rights**. This relationship allowed patrollers to act with impunity, as they were backed by the **legal authority** of the local government.

Furthermore, local authorities benefited from the slave patrol system by relying on patrollers to uphold the **existing social hierarchy** and prevent **slave uprisings** or escapes. By delegating the responsibility of slave control to the patrollers, local authorities could focus on other aspects of governance and economic pursuits. In return, patrollers received validation and reinforcement of their power, creating a system where both parties depended on each other for maintaining control over the enslaved population.

Resistance and Opposition to Patrols

Amid the **structured system of slave patrols** in the Southern colonies, instances of **resistance and opposition** to the patrols emerged as **enslaved individuals and communities** challenged the oppressive surveillance and control imposed upon them. Enslaved people employed various tactics to resist the patrols, such as running away, hiding, or engaging in acts of sabotage. Some would feign illness or injury to avoid being subjected to the patrols' scrutiny, while others would strategically mislead or outsmart patrollers to evade capture.

Additionally, enslaved communities often banded together to support those attempting to escape or resist capture, demonstrating **solidarity and collective resistance** against the patrols' authority. These **acts of resistance** were not only a means of **asserting autonomy** and resisting oppression but also served as a form of **survival strategy** for enslaved individuals facing **constant surveillance and control**. The persistent efforts to undermine the effectiveness of slave patrols highlight the resilience and resourcefulness of those subjected to such oppressive systems in the Southern colonies.

Impact on Enslaved Communities

Impact on Enslaved Communities can be seen through the lens of how the systematic presence of **slave patrols** influenced daily life and interactions within these **marginalized groups**. The establishment of formalized slave patrols in the Southern Colonies had profound effects on enslaved communities. The constant fear of being apprehended by patrollers while attempting to escape or simply going about their **daily activities** created a pervasive atmosphere of **surveillance and control**. This led to **heightened levels of anxiety** and restricted freedom of movement for the enslaved individuals, impacting their ability to resist or challenge the institution of slavery.

Moreover, the presence of slave patrols further exacerbated the **power dynamics** within enslaved communities. The patrols not only enforced labor discipline but also instilled a sense of mistrust and division among the enslaved population. This **internal strife** hindered **collective resistance efforts** and solidarity among the enslaved, making it more challenging to organize revolts or uprisings against their oppressors. The psychological toll of living under constant surveillance and the threat of punishment by patrollers contributed to the perpetuation of a system that sought to **dehumanize and subjugate** enslaved individuals.

Legacy of Slave Patrols Today

Within contemporary society, the enduring legacy of **slave patrols** persists in shaping social structures and attitudes towards marginalized communities. The historical roots of **systemic racism** and oppression that were perpetuated by slave patrols have left a lasting impact on modern-day **law enforcement practices** and community relations. The disproportionate targeting and mistreatment of Black individuals by law enforcement, evidenced by higher rates of **police brutality** and incarceration, can be traced back to the **dehumanizing tactics** employed by slave patrols to control and oppress enslaved people.

Moreover, the deep-seated biases and prejudices that were ingrained in the mindset of slave patrollers continue to influence **societal perceptions** of marginalized communities today. This legacy of suspicion and hostility towards people of color contributes to ongoing **racial disparities** in areas such as education, employment, and healthcare. By acknowledging and understanding the historical context of slave patrols, we can begin to address the **systemic injustices** that persist in our society and work towards creating a more equitable and inclusive future.

Conclusion and Key Takeaways

Certainly, the examination of the **legacy of slave patrols** reveals profound insights into the **systemic inequalities** and injustices that persist in contemporary society. The formalization of slave patrols in the Southern Colonies laid the foundation for the **deeply rooted racial biases** and discriminatory practices that continue to shape social structures today.

The oppressive tactics employed by these patrols, such as surveillance, violence, and control, have seeped into **modern law enforcement practices**, contributing to the **disproportionate targeting** and mistreatment of marginalized communities, particularly people of color.

Moreover, the significance of using **state-sanctioned violence** to maintain power and uphold oppressive systems has perpetuated a cycle of mistrust and fear between law enforcement agencies and communities they are meant to serve. Acknowledging this history is imperative in understanding the complexities of **current social issues**, such as police brutality, racial profiling, and mass incarceration.

Conclusion

To sum up, the emergence of **formalized slave patrols** in the southern colonies represented a significant turning point in the enforcement of slavery. These patrols served as a tool of control and surveillance over enslaved individuals, perpetuating **systems of oppression** and exploitation.

Despite resistance and opposition, the legacy of slave patrols continues to impact communities today, highlighting the **enduring effects** of **historical injustices**.

The study of this dark chapter in American history underscores the importance of understanding our past to shape a more just future.

Legal Foundations and Mandates for Slave Patrols

Colonial-era laws in the United States authorized **slave patrols**, empowering white men to enforce discipline and prevent uprisings among enslaved populations. State laws like the **1704 South Carolina Slave Code** mandated patrols, institutionalizing control and reinforcing **racial hierarchies**. Slave codes assigned specific duties to patrols, such as apprehending runaways and suppressing rebellions, under the authority of the colonial government. The role of **local magistrates** was crucial in overseeing patrol operations and enforcing regulations. Enforcement of curfews and passes restricted enslaved individuals' movements, with **severe punishments** for non-compliance. Understanding these legal foundations highlights the oppressive nature of slavery.

Key Takeaways

- Colonial laws authorized slave patrols to enforce discipline and prevent uprisings.
- Patrols were composed of white property-owning men, reinforcing racial hierarchies.
- State laws like the 1704 South Carolina Slave Code mandated patrol duties.
- Patrols enforced curfews, passes, and state laws to control enslaved populations.
- Magistrates oversaw patrols, resolving disputes and enforcing regulations on enslaved

individuals.

Colonial Era Legal Authorization

During the **Colonial Era**, the **legal authorization** for **slave patrols** was firmly established within the framework of local and **state laws**, providing a foundation for the systematic monitoring and control of enslaved populations. These laws granted slave patrols the authority to enforce discipline, prevent uprisings, and **maintain the status quo** of slavery. The patrols were typically composed of **white men**, often with the requirement that they own a certain amount of property, and were tasked with monitoring the movements and activities of enslaved individuals.

State statutes in the Southern colonies, such as the 1704 **South Carolina Slave Code**, explicitly mandated the creation and operation of slave patrols. These laws outlined the duties and responsibilities of patrollers, including the power to apprehend and punish enslaved individuals found engaging in unauthorized activities. The legal framework surrounding slave patrols not only institutionalized the control of enslaved populations but also reinforced the **racial hierarchies** and power dynamics of the time.

This legal foundation laid the groundwork for the development of more detailed regulations and practices governing slave patrols in the subsequent years.

Slave Codes and Patrol Duties

Within the legal framework of the Southern colonies, **slave codes** delineated specific duties and responsibilities assigned to **slave patrols**, solidifying their role in maintaining control over enslaved populations. These codes were a set of laws enacted to regulate the institution of slavery, with a particular focus on the behavior and movements of enslaved individuals. Slave patrols, comprised of white men often drawn from the **local militias**, were tasked with enforcing these codes and ensuring that slaves did not attempt to escape or engage in any activities deemed rebellious or threatening to the established order.

The slave patrols operated under the authority of the colonial governments, embodying the **state-sanctioned oppression** of enslaved people. Their duties included conducting regular patrols, apprehending **runaways**, suppressing **slave rebellions**, and monitoring the interactions between slaves and **free individuals**. The enforcement of slave codes through patrols created a pervasive atmosphere of fear and control among the enslaved population, reinforcing their subjugation and further entrenching the **power dynamics** of the slave society.

State Legislation on Patrolling

Enacting specific **state legislation**, governments in the Southern colonies institutionalized the **duties and authority** of **slave patrols**, further cementing their role in regulating and controlling the enslaved population. These laws empowered patrols to monitor the movements of enslaved individuals, prevent gatherings, and use force if necessary. For example, in **South Carolina**, the **Negro Act of 1740** required white men to serve in the patrol units and granted them broad powers to **search any slave premises** and apprehend runaways. Similarly, Virginia's slave patrol laws mandated regular patrols and imposed fines on patrol members who neglected their duties.

State legislation on patrolling not only **formalized the existence** of slave patrols but also provided legal backing for their actions. These laws not only reinforced the oppressive nature of slavery but also served to maintain social order and uphold the **economic interests** of slaveholders. The codification of patrol duties in state statutes solidified the control exerted over the enslaved population and contributed to the perpetuation of the institution of slavery in the Southern colonies.

Role of Local Magistrates

Local magistrates played a significant role in overseeing and enforcing the regulations established by **state legislation** regarding slave patrols in the Southern colonies. These magistrates were responsible for appointing **patrol leaders**, allocating resources, and guaranteeing patrols operated within the legal framework. They held the authority to issue warrants for searches, seizures, and arrests related to **suspected slave insurrections** or unlawful activities. Magistrates also presided over **trials involving enslaved individuals** accused of misconduct or attempting to escape.

Moreover, local magistrates were tasked with **resolving disputes between patrol members** and slave owners, as well as addressing complaints from the general public regarding the conduct of patrols. They were instrumental in **maintaining order** and upholding the institution of slavery by **enforcing curfews**, passes, and other restrictions imposed on enslaved populations. The magistrates' close supervision of these patrols helped ensure that state laws were enforced consistently and that the interests of slaveholders were protected.

Enforcing Curfews and Passes

The strict enforcement of **curfews** and **passes** formed a key aspect of the **operational protocols** overseen by local magistrates in the context of slave patrols in the Southern colonies. Curfews were imposed to restrict the movement of enslaved individuals during nighttime hours, aiming to prevent gatherings or potential escapes. Enslaved persons were required to carry passes when traveling outside the plantation or designated areas, detailing their owner's permission and purpose for being off-premises. This system enabled **patrol officers** to stop any enslaved person they encountered and demand to see their pass, ensuring compliance with regulations.

The enforcement of curfews and passes served to maintain control over the enslaved population, reinforcing the **power dynamics** of slavery. Failure to adhere to these regulations often resulted in **severe punishments**, highlighting the strict oversight and **surveillance** imposed by slave patrols. Additionally, these measures instilled fear among enslaved individuals, further perpetuating their subjugation and limiting opportunities for resistance or autonomy. The systematic enforcement of curfews and passes underscored the pervasive nature of surveillance and control within the **institution of slavery**.

Punishments for Enslaved Individuals

Punishments meted out to enslaved individuals within the context of **slave patrols** were characterized by severity and served as a means of asserting control and discipline. Enslaved individuals faced a range of **harsh penalties** for perceived transgressions, with **whipping** being one of the most common forms of punishment. Whippings were often administered publicly as a means of **instilling fear** and **demonstrating authority**. In addition to physical punishments, enslaved individuals could also face more **insidious forms of retribution**, such as being sold away from their families or subjected to prolonged periods of solitary confinement.

The severity of punishments was intended to deter resistance and reinforce the **power dynamics** inherent in the institution of slavery. By subjecting enslaved individuals to brutal and dehumanizing forms of punishment, slave patrols aimed to maintain order and quash any potential acts of rebellion. These punitive measures not only inflicted physical harm but also served to remind enslaved individuals of their subservient status within the oppressive system of slavery.

Militarization of Patrols

The evolution of **slave patrols** saw a notable shift towards a more **militarized approach** in their operations, reflecting a systematic escalation in the **enforcement mechanisms** utilized to control enslaved individuals. As the institution of slavery expanded in the United States, slave patrols increasingly adopted military tactics and structures. Patrols began to resemble **paramilitary units**, with organized formations, **hierarchical command structures**, and the use of **military-grade equipment** such as firearms, horses, and sometimes even small cannons. This militarization was not only aimed at maintaining control over enslaved populations but also served as a deterrent to potential uprisings or escape attempts.

The militarization of patrols had profound implications for enslaved communities, intensifying the **atmosphere of fear** and oppression. The presence of heavily armed patrols heightened the sense of surveillance and vulnerability among the enslaved population, reinforcing the **power dynamics** of slavery. The use of military force by patrols also symbolized the underlying violence and coercion that underpinned the slave system, perpetuating a cycle of subjugation and resistance.

Interactions with Enslaved Communities

Within the context of slave patrols' operations, interactions with enslaved communities were characterized by a pervasive atmosphere of **control and surveillance**. Patrols were tasked with **maintaining order**, preventing uprisings, and **enforcing the strict regulations** imposed on enslaved individuals.

Patrol members often employed **intimidation tactics**, such as regular patrols through plantations, random searches of enslaved quarters, and frequent interrogations, to instill fear and deter any potential resistance. Enslaved individuals lived under **constant scrutiny**, with patrols monitoring their movements, interactions, and activities.

Any perceived disobedience or defiance was met with **swift and severe punishment**, reinforcing the power dynamics and hierarchies of the time. These interactions were marked by a lack of autonomy for the enslaved population, who faced constant intrusion into their daily lives by the patrols.

The presence of patrols created a **climate of fear** and oppression, further entrenching the institution of slavery and perpetuating the dehumanization of enslaved individuals.

Legacy of Slave Patrol Laws

The enduring legacy of **slave patrol laws** continues to shape contemporary perceptions of law enforcement practices in the United States and influence discussions surrounding **systemic racism**. These laws, which date back to the early 18th century, were designed to maintain control over enslaved populations and protect the interests of slave owners. While the formal abolition of slavery occurred with the ratification of the 13th Amendment in 1865, the principles and tactics employed by slave patrols persisted, evolving into **modern policing methods**.

The legacy of slave patrol laws is evident in the disproportionate targeting of minority communities by law enforcement, leading to concerns about **racial profiling** and **discriminatory practices**. The historical context of these laws underscores the deep-rooted issues within the **criminal justice system** and highlights the need for reform to address systemic racism. By acknowledging the **historical underpinnings** of modern law enforcement, society can work towards creating a more equitable and just system that upholds the rights and dignity of all individuals.

Conclusion

To sum up, the **legal foundations** and mandates for slave patrols in the colonial era were deeply rooted in the **dehumanization and control** of enslaved individuals. These laws symbolize the systematic oppression and violence that pervaded American society, leaving a **lasting legacy** of trauma and inequality.

The militarization and enforcement tactics employed by slave patrols served to maintain a system of subjugation and fear, perpetuating a history of injustice that continues to impact communities to this day.

CHAPTER 3: FUNCTIONS AND OPERATIONS OF SLAVE PATROLS

Roles and Responsibilities of Slave Patrol Members

Slave patrol members in the American South were responsible for **enforcing slave codes**, **preventing rebellions**, and **upholding the institution** of slavery. They surveilled and controlled enslaved individuals, collaborated with local authorities, and reinforced racial hierarchy. Their role in maintaining social control and oppression was instrumental in the systemic perpetuation of slavery. By understanding their roles and responsibilities, one can grasp the significant impact these patrols had on shaping historical practices that continue to influence modern policing approaches.

Key Takeaways

- Enforcing slave codes to regulate behavior and movements of enslaved individuals.
- Monitoring and controlling the movements of enslaved individuals to prevent uprisings.
- Acting as a form of social control to maintain the institution of slavery.
- Collaborating with local authorities to uphold the interests of slave owners.
- Contributing to the perpetuation of racial hierarchy and oppression.

Formation and Organization

With the establishment of **slave patrols** serving as a foundational element in the enforcement of control over enslaved populations, understanding the formation and organization of these groups is essential in comprehending their role in maintaining the system of slavery in the American South.

Slave patrols were typically organized at the local level, consisting of white men, often **wealthy landowners** or those with social status, who were tasked with monitoring and controlling the movements of enslaved individuals. These patrols were **officially sanctioned** by colonial and state governments, providing legal authority to **patrol members** to stop, search, and apprehend any enslaved person found to be violating laws or social norms.

The **hierarchical structure** within these patrols often mirrored military organizations, with **designated leaders** overseeing the activities of patrol members.

Surveillance and Monitoring Duties

Amidst the **oppressive system of slavery** in the American South, the **surveillance and monitoring duties** undertaken by **slave patrol members** played an important role in maintaining control over enslaved populations.

These patrols, often composed of white men, were tasked with overseeing the movements and activities of enslaved individuals. Patrol members would regularly conduct patrols on plantations, roads, and public spaces to **prevent any potential uprisings** or attempts at escape. They closely monitored the interactions between enslaved individuals, ensuring compliance with slave codes and preventing any form of resistance.

This **constant surveillance instilled fear** and deterred acts of defiance among the enslaved population, contributing significantly to the perpetuation of the slave system in the South.

Apprehension and Punishment

Enforcing **harsh repercussions** for perceived infractions, **slave patrol members** diligently carried out the tasks of apprehension and punishment within the oppressive slave system in the American South. These patrols, often composed of white men deputized to police enslaved populations, were responsible for capturing and **disciplining individuals attempting to escape** bondage or those deemed to be breaking plantation rules.

Apprehension methods included tracking, using bloodhounds, and conducting searches of homes and surrounding areas. Punishments for captured individuals varied but were consistently severe, ranging from **physical beatings** to being sold to **harsher masters** or even death. The role of slave patrols in **maintaining control through apprehension** and punishment was a fundamental aspect of the brutal enforcement of the institution of slavery in the antebellum South.

Enforcement of Slave Codes

The enforcement of **slave codes** further entrenched the power dynamics and **control mechanisms** wielded by **slave patrol members** in the American South during the era of slavery. Slave codes were laws that **regulated the behavior** of enslaved individuals and **restricted their movements**, activities, and rights. Slave patrol members played an essential role in ensuring these codes were strictly enforced.

They patrolled plantations, public spaces, and roads to monitor and control the movements of enslaved people. Patrol members were authorized to stop, interrogate, and use force against any enslaved person found violating the codes. By actively **enforcing these oppressive laws**, slave patrol members perpetuated the dehumanization and exploitation of enslaved individuals, reinforcing the system of slavery in the American South.

Collaboration with Slave Owners

In fostering a symbiotic relationship aimed at maintaining control and reinforcing the institution of slavery, **slave patrol members** closely collaborated with **slave owners** in the American South.

Slave patrols often relied on information provided by slave owners regarding **potential escape attempts**, rebellions, or instances of **disobedience among the enslaved individuals**. This collaboration extended to the **sharing of resources** such as weapons, horses, and manpower, enabling slave patrols to effectively carry out their duties of surveillance and control.

Additionally, slave owners would call upon patrol members to assist in **capturing and punishing runaway slaves**, further solidifying their partnership. This collaboration between slave patrol members and slave owners was instrumental in upholding the oppressive system of slavery in the antebellum South.

Patrolling Plantations and Roads

Patrolling the vast expanses of plantations and meandering roads, **slave patrol members** diligently monitored and controlled the movements of enslaved individuals in the American South. These patrols were essential in **maintaining the oppressive system** of slavery by instilling fear, **preventing escapes**, and **enforcing labor discipline**.

Plantations, where the majority of enslaved individuals worked, required constant surveillance to prevent rebellions and guarantee continuous labor. The patrols also extended their monitoring to the roads, as they served as potential escape routes for enslaved individuals seeking freedom.

Role in Preventing Slave Rebellions

Slave patrol members played an important role in maintaining the oppressive system of slavery by actively working to **prevent slave rebellions** through **constant surveillance** and enforcement of discipline. These patrols, consisting of **armed white men**, were tasked with monitoring the movements and behaviors of enslaved individuals to quash any potential uprisings.

Patrol members would conduct regular inspections of plantations, searching for hidden weapons, monitoring communication between slaves, and punishing any signs of resistance harshly. Their presence instilled fear among the enslaved population, discouraging **organized rebellions** and ensuring the continued subjugation of individuals held in bondage.

Relationship with Local Authorities

With an intricate web of communication and collaboration, **slave patrol members** established a symbiotic relationship with local authorities to uphold the institution of slavery. These patrols often worked hand in hand with **local law enforcement officials**, sheriffs, and other government representatives to **enforce laws** that regulated the movements and behaviors of enslaved individuals.

Local authorities provided **legal backing** and legitimacy to the actions of slave patrols, granting them the power to detain, search, and punish enslaved individuals. In return, slave patrol members assisted local authorities in maintaining **social order** and ensuring the stability of the slave system.

This close relationship between slave patrols and local authorities reinforced the oppressive nature of slavery and further entrenched the control of **slaveholders** over the enslaved population.

Legacy and Impact

The enduring legacy and far-reaching impact of the **collaboration between slave patrol members** and local authorities reverberates through the annals of history, **shaping societal structures and attitudes** towards law enforcement and race relations.

This collaboration laid the foundation for the **development of modern policing** in the United States, with many of the tactics and strategies employed by slave patrols being incorporated into law enforcement practices.

The legacy of this relationship is evident in the **racial disparities** that persist in the criminal justice system today, highlighting the deep-rooted nature of **systemic racism**.

Additionally, the historical association between law enforcement and the **subjugation of marginalized communities** continues to influence perceptions of police legitimacy and trust within these communities, emphasizing the importance of acknowledging and addressing this legacy in contemporary discussions on policing and race.

Conclusion

To sum up, the **roles and responsibilities** of slave patrol members were deeply embedded in the enforcement of slavery and the control of enslaved individuals. Their **surveillance, apprehension, and enforcement** duties were vital in maintaining the oppressive system of slavery.

The legacy of slave patrols continues to impact society today, serving as a reminder of the **systemic racism** and injustice that has shaped our history.

Tactics and Methods Employed by Slave Patrols

Slave patrols employed regular patrols, informants, tracking dogs, and **surveillance techniques** to instill fear and prevent uprisings. They relied on **networks of informants**, search parties, and checkpoints to capture escapees. Punitive measures enforced labor quotas, curfews, and dominance. Communication was key through signals and collaboration with local militias. Firearm, whips, and horses were used for control. The impact led to fear, trauma, helplessness, and **intergenerational trauma**. **Slave patrols** upheld slavery through racial hierarchies, violence, and economic interests. The system of control and oppression went beyond physical boundaries.

Key Takeaways

- Regular patrols on foot and horseback to maintain visibility and control.
- Utilization of informants and tracking dogs for surveillance and capture.
- Punitive measures like physical abuse and curfews to assert dominance.
- Communication through signals and coordination with local militias and plantation owners.
- Use of firearms, whips, and horses to instill fear and maintain control over enslaved individuals.

Patrolling and Surveillance Techniques

In the context of **slave patrols**, patrolling and **surveillance techniques** were meticulously designed and executed to maintain a constant presence and control over enslaved individuals within their designated territories.

Patrollers utilized various methods such as regular patrols on horseback or foot, with specific routes and schedule to maximize visibility. Surveillance was also conducted through informants within the enslaved community, who provided information on any potential resistance or escape plans.

Additionally, patrols often employed **tracking dogs** to assist in locating runaway slaves. The goal of these techniques was to establish fear, **prevent rebellions**, and guarantee the **continuous subjugation** of the enslaved population.

Through these systematic approaches, slave patrols sought to reinforce the oppressive system of slavery in the **antebellum South**.

Capture and Apprehension Methods

Continuing the enforcement strategies employed by **slave patrols**, the capture and apprehension methods utilized were carefully devised to swiftly and effectively secure individuals attempting to escape bondage. Slave patrols often relied on a **network of informants** within the enslaved community to gather intelligence on potential escapees.

Once a runaway was identified, patrols would organize search parties, utilizing **tracking dogs and horses** to pursue and capture the individual. In some cases, patrols would set up **checkpoints along known escape routes** or at strategic locations to intercept fleeing individuals. These capture methods were designed to **instill fear** among the enslaved population and deter future escape attempts.

The systematic and calculated approach of slave patrols ensured a **high success rate** in apprehending those seeking freedom.

Punishment and Deterrence Measures

Employing a range of **punitive measures** and **deterrent tactics**, slave patrols aimed to maintain control over the enslaved population and suppress any notions of resistance or rebellion. Punishments varied from **physical abuse** such as whipping, branding, and even mutilation, to **psychological tactics** like public humiliation and isolation. These measures were intended not only to punish individuals but also to serve as a warning to others, emphasizing the consequences of disobedience.

Deterrence strategies included regular patrols, curfews, and strict enforcement of **labor quotas**, instilling fear and discouraging any thoughts of escape or rebellion. By utilizing a combination of punishment and deterrence, slave patrols sought to assert dominance and control over enslaved individuals, perpetuating the **oppressive system** of slavery.

Communication and Coordination Strategies

Utilizing **effective communication channels** and strategic coordination methods was essential for slave patrols to efficiently monitor and control the movements and activities of the enslaved population. Communication among patrol members was often facilitated through **signals like horn blowing**, drum beating, or specific codes. These signals conveyed messages about the location of enslaved individuals, potential uprisings, or any suspicious activities.

Coordination strategies involved dividing patrol units into smaller groups, each responsible for a specific area and establishing **predetermined meeting points** in case of emergencies. Additionally, slave patrols often collaborated with **local militias, plantation owners**, and community members to enhance surveillance efforts. This network allowed for the **rapid dissemination of information** and the swift mobilization of forces when needed.

Weapons and Equipment Utilized

Amidst their duties to enforce control over enslaved individuals, slave patrols relied on a variety of weapons and equipment to carry out their surveillance and apprehension tasks efficiently. Commonly used weapons included **firearms** such as muskets, rifles, and pistols, providing the patrols with means to intimidate and use force if needed.

Additionally, patrols utilized **whips**, batons, and **ropes** to physically restrain and subdue individuals. **Horses** were an essential part of their equipment, enabling patrols to cover large areas quickly and effectively chase down runaways. Some patrols also employed **bloodhounds** to track and capture escapees.

The combination of these weapons and equipment granted slave patrols the tools necessary to maintain dominance and control over enslaved populations.

Legal Authority and Regulations

Slave patrols operated under specific **legal authority** and regulations that dictated their scope of power and actions within the societal framework of that time. These patrols were typically authorized by colonial or state governments and were tasked with **enforcing slave codes** and **maintaining control** over enslaved populations.

The legal framework surrounding **slave patrols** varied across regions, but common regulations included the ability to **stop, search, and detain** any enslaved individual without a warrant. Slave patrols were often empowered to use violence to guarantee compliance and prevent insurrections, with **legal immunity** granted to patrol members in many cases.

The regulations governing slave patrols served to institutionalize the control and oppression of enslaved individuals, reinforcing the power dynamics of the time.

Interactions with Enslaved Individuals

In their interactions with enslaved individuals, patrol members often employed **intimidation tactics** and **strict enforcement measures** to maintain control and uphold the hierarchical power structure of the time. Patrols would frequently use **fear-inducing methods** such as public punishments, verbal abuse, and physical violence to assert dominance over enslaved individuals and deter any thoughts of resistance or escape.

Patrol members would conduct **routine inspections** of plantations, questioning and searching enslaved individuals to guarantee compliance with regulations and to instill a sense of **constant surveillance**. These interactions were marked by a clear display of authority and a reinforcement of the subordinate status of the enslaved population, highlighting the oppressive nature of the slave patrol system.

Training and Recruitment Procedures

The process of selecting and training individuals for **slave patrol duty** involved rigorous assessments and instruction to guarantee a proficient and disciplined enforcement unit.

Prospective patrol members were often chosen from the white male population, with a focus on **physical fitness**, **marksmanship skills**, and loyalty to the plantation owners.

Training programs included teachings on tracking techniques, weapon proficiency, and methods of surveillance. Recruits were also educated on the **legal powers** they held over enslaved individuals and the consequences of **insubordination**.

Training sessions aimed to instill a sense of duty, obedience, and a commitment to maintaining the established social order. The thorough recruitment and **training procedures** were designed to create a cohesive and effective slave patrol force.

Impact on Enslaved Communities

The presence of **slave patrols** within plantation societies had profound, far-reaching ramifications on the enslaved communities they governed. These patrols instilled fear, restricted movement, and enforced **harsh discipline**, perpetuating a system of control and oppression.

Enslaved individuals lived in constant apprehension of being caught, punished, or even killed by patrollers, leading to **heightened levels of stress** and anxiety. The patrols' presence also **disrupted familial and social bonds** within enslaved communities, as individuals were often separated, leading to a **loss of cultural identity** and heritage.

Additionally, the psychological trauma inflicted by the constant surveillance and **threat of violence** lingered long after patrols disbanded, leaving lasting scars on generations of enslaved people and their descendants.

Conclusion

To sum up, the tactics and methods employed by slave patrols were characterized by **ruthless efficiency** and systematic oppression.

Through their patrolling and surveillance techniques, **capture and apprehension** methods,

punishment and deterrence measures, communication and coordination strategies, weapons and equipment utilization, legal authority and regulations, interactions with enslaved individuals, **training and recruitment** procedures, and overall impact on enslaved communities, slave patrols maintained a tight grip on the enslaved population, perpetuating fear and control on a massive scale.

Relationship between Slave Patrols and Plantation Owners

The relationship between **slave patrols** and **plantation owners** in the United States was multifaceted. Slave patrols enforced discipline, often using violence, at the behest of plantation owners to **maintain control** and protect **economic interests**. This collaboration secured obedience and productivity within Southern colonial societies. The power dynamics and social hierarchy created by this relationship were instrumental in perpetuating **systemic racism** and inequalities. Understanding this historical context sheds light on modern racial dynamics and challenges. The complexities of this relationship reveal a deeper understanding of the intertwined histories of enforcement, control, and economic interests in the Southern colonies.

Key Takeaways

- Plantation owners relied on slave patrols to maintain control and discipline over enslaved populations.
- Slave patrols enforced the interests of plantation owners through violence, intimidation, and punishment.
- Collaboration between owners and patrols ensured obedience and productivity in plantation societies.
- The relationship between owners and patrols was symbiotic, reinforcing the power dynamics within plantations.
- Slave patrols and plantation owners worked together to protect the economic interests of the plantation system.

Formation of Plantation Societies

In examining the historical context of the Southern colonies, the establishment and evolution of **plantation societies** were intricately intertwined with the economic reliance on **enslaved labor**. Plantation societies emerged as large-scale agricultural enterprises, primarily cultivating **cash crops** such as tobacco, rice, and cotton.

These plantations were typically owned by **wealthy landowners** who utilized enslaved labor to maximize profits. The **labor-intensive** nature of cash crop cultivation necessitated a significant workforce, leading to the widespread use of enslaved individuals.

As plantation societies grew, they shaped the economic, social, and political landscape of the Southern colonies, contributing to the consolidation of wealth and power among a small elite class. The reliance on enslaved labor within these societies laid the foundation for the **systemic oppression** and exploitation that persisted for generations.

Role of Slave Patrols in Enforcing Discipline

Slave patrols operated as organized groups tasked with **maintaining discipline and control** over enslaved populations in the Southern colonies. These patrols were essential for plantation owners to guarantee the obedience of their **enslaved workforce**.

Patrol members, often white men from the local community, were responsible for monitoring the movements and behaviors of the enslaved individuals. They had the **authority to use violence**, intimidation, and punishment to enforce discipline and **prevent any attempts at rebellion** or escape.

The presence of **slave patrols** instilled fear among the enslaved population, **reinforcing the power**

dynamics within the plantation societies. The systematic enforcement of rules and regulations through these patrols contributed notably to the oppressive and dehumanizing conditions experienced by the enslaved individuals.

Collaboration in Maintaining Control

Evident through **historical records** and accounts, the **collaboration** between **plantation owners** and **slave patrols** reinforced **control over the enslaved population** in the Southern colonies. Plantation owners relied on slave patrols to monitor and suppress any signs of **rebellion or resistance** among the enslaved individuals. By working together, plantation owners provided the authority and resources necessary for slave patrols to operate effectively.

In return, slave patrols guaranteed that enslaved individuals followed plantation rules and maintained order, thereby safeguarding the economic interests of the plantation owners. This collaboration created a system where both parties benefited from each other's actions, ultimately solidifying control over the enslaved population and perpetuating the oppressive system of slavery in the Southern colonies.

Protection of Plantation Interests

The **symbiotic relationship** between plantation owners and **slave patrols** was intricately woven to safeguard and promote the **economic interests** inherent in the plantation system. Plantation owners relied on slave patrols to maintain control over enslaved populations, ensuring that their labor force remained intact and productive.

In return, slave patrols received support and authority from the plantation owners to carry out their duties effectively. The patrols were tasked with preventing slave revolts, escapes, and uprisings that could threaten the profitability of the **plantations**.

Influence of Economic Incentives

In considering the dynamics between **plantation owners** and **slave patrols**, it becomes evident that **economic incentives** played a pivotal role in shaping their collaborative relationship. Plantation owners relied on slave patrols to **safeguard their investments** in enslaved labor. These patrols guaranteed that enslaved individuals remained under control, preventing potential uprisings or escapes that could jeopardize the economic productivity of the plantation.

In return, **slave patrol members** received compensation, either through direct payment or other benefits such as land grants or social status elevation. The economic interests of plantation owners aligned with the goals of slave patrols, creating a symbiotic relationship where both parties benefited financially. This **mutual dependency** further solidified the bond between plantation owners and slave patrols, emphasizing the significant role of economic incentives in shaping their association.

Power Dynamics and Social Hierarchy

The hierarchical structure between **plantation owners** and **slave patrols** was intricately intertwined with **power dynamics** that perpetuated the **social order** within the institution of slavery. Plantation owners held the ultimate authority within this system, exercising control over both the enslaved individuals and the patrols that monitored them.

The owners' economic wealth and social status solidified their dominance, shaping power dynamics that extended beyond the economic sphere. Slave patrols, primarily composed of poor whites, were tasked with enforcing the owners' interests, thereby reinforcing the existing **social hierarchy**.

This relationship created a power dynamic that maintained the subjugation of enslaved individuals while reinforcing the authority and control of plantation owners. The intersection of power, social hierarchy, and control was central to perpetuating the **oppressive system** of slavery.

Resistance and Rebellions

Amidst the **oppressive system of slavery**, **acts of resistance** and rebellions were a proof of the **unwavering spirit** and defiance of the enslaved individuals against their subjugation. Enslaved individuals engaged in various forms of resistance, such as sabotaging plantation work, feigning illness, and escaping to freedom through networks like the **Underground Railroad**.

Rebellions, such as Nat Turner's Rebellion in 1831 and the **Stono Rebellion** in 1739, stand as powerful examples of enslaved people's refusal to accept their circumstances. These acts of resistance and rebellion were not only attempts to secure freedom but also served as challenges to the **dehumanizing institution** of slavery. They demonstrated the enslaved individuals' agency and determination to resist their oppressors despite the grave risks involved.

Legacy of Slave Patrols

Slave patrols, also known as patrollers, were organized groups tasked with monitoring and controlling enslaved individuals in the **Southern United States**. The significance of **slave patrols** continues to have **lasting effects on American society**.

These patrols laid the **foundation for modern policing** in the United States, with many law enforcement agencies tracing their origins back to these patrols. The tactics and strategies employed by patrollers, such as surveillance, intimidation, and violence, have perpetuated **racial biases and inequalities** in the criminal justice system.

The distrust and fear of law enforcement among minority communities can be linked to the historical oppression and brutality experienced under slave patrols. Understanding this legacy is vital in addressing **systemic racism** and working towards a more equitable society.

Implications for Modern Racial Dynamics

Examining the historical relationship between **slave patrols** and **plantation owners** sheds light on the complex dynamics that continue to shape modern racial inequalities. The legacy of these systems has had lasting effects on contemporary racial dynamics.

The power dynamics and **racial hierarchies** established during the era of slavery have persisted, albeit in more subtle forms, in modern society. The **disproportionate incarceration rates** of Black individuals, racial profiling by law enforcement and **systemic inequalities** in education and employment can all be linked back to the historical foundations laid by slave patrols and plantation owners.

Understanding these implications is vital for addressing and dismantling the systemic racism that persists in various aspects of society today.

Conclusion

To sum up, the relationship between **slave patrols** and **plantation owners** was characterized by **collaboration and mutual benefit**.

While some may argue that slave patrols were necessary for maintaining control and protecting plantation interests, it is important to acknowledge the oppressive and violent nature of their role in enforcing discipline and upholding the power dynamics of the social hierarchy.

The legacy of slave patrols continues to impact **modern racial dynamics**, highlighting the lasting effects of this historical relationship.

Slave Patrols and the Expansion of the Plantation Economy in the Antebellum South

Slave patrols in the **Antebellum South** were vital for expanding the **plantation economy**. They controlled and exploited **enslaved labor**, aligning with plantation owners' economic interests. Through surveillance and coercion, patrols guaranteed profitability by maintaining **labor discipline**. Enslaved individuals faced dehumanization and harsh conditions, sustaining the plantation system's dominance. The patrols' role in **economic prosperity** highlights the deep-rooted connection between labor control and financial gain in this era. Understanding this intricate dynamic provides insight into the systemic oppression that characterized the antebellum South. Further insights wait on the impact and legacy of these practices.

Key Takeaways

- Slave patrols ensured labor control and minimized insurrection risks on plantations.
- They safeguarded investments and increased efficiency of labor extraction through fear.
- Discipline and punishment enforced by patrols secured economic interests in the antebellum South.
- Patrols contributed to the expansion of the plantation system by maintaining profitability.
- Connection to economic prosperity highlighted the role of patrols in financial gain and control.

Enforcement of Slave Labor on Plantations

Enforcing **slave labor** on plantations involved a complex system of **surveillance**, **punishment**, and **coercion** to guarantee maximum productivity and profitability for the slave-owning elite. Plantation owners utilized **overseers** to monitor enslaved individuals closely, often resorting to **violent methods** to assure compliance. Whippings, physical restraints, and other forms of punishment were common tactics employed to maintain control and discipline among the enslaved workforce. The threat of **separation from family members** or the sale of individuals to harsher plantations also served as powerful tools to compel obedience and hard labor.

Furthermore, the plantation economy relied heavily on the **exploitation of enslaved labor** for its sustenance and growth. Enslaved individuals were forced to toil in harsh conditions for long hours, with little to no respite. The profitability of plantations was intricately linked to the exploitation of the physical and mental labor of the enslaved population. This oppressive system not only perpetuated the dehumanization of enslaved individuals but also entrenched the power dynamics that underpinned the antebellum South's economic prosperity.

Impact on Enslaved Communities

The enduring repercussions of the **stringent enforcement** of **slave labor** on plantations reverberated deeply within the fabric of enslaved communities, shaping their social structures and individual experiences in profound ways. Enslaved communities faced relentless exploitation and **dehumanization**, leading to the erosion of **familial bonds** as members was frequently separated through sales or punishment. This disruption of kinship networks not only caused immense emotional distress but also hindered the transmission of **cultural heritage** and traditions, impacting the collective identity of enslaved individuals.

Moreover, the constant surveillance and control imposed by **slave patrols** instilled fear and apprehension within enslaved communities, creating a climate of **perpetual insecurity** and vulnerability. This pervasive atmosphere of terror served to suppress any attempts at **resistance or rebellion**, further solidifying the power dynamics that upheld the institution of slavery. Additionally, the harsh living conditions and brutal treatment endured by the enslaved population resulted in physical and psychological trauma that persisted long after emancipation, underscoring the **enduring legacy** of oppression and injustice faced by enslaved communities in the antebellum South.

Role in Maintaining Social Order

Slave patrols played a pivotal role in upholding **social order** in the **antebellum South** through their systematic **surveillance** and enforcement mechanisms within the **plantation economy**. These patrols, consisting of white men often deputized by local governments, were responsible for monitoring **enslaved populations**, preventing revolts, and capturing runaway slaves.

By maintaining a constant presence on plantations, **slave patrols** instilled fear and submission among the enslaved community, reinforcing the **power dynamics** of the time. Their mere existence served as a form of social control, reminding enslaved individuals of the consequences of disobedience. The patrols also acted as a visible symbol of authority, embodying the oppressive nature of the institution of slavery.

Additionally, their activities extended beyond plantations, patrolling public spaces to regulate the movements of both enslaved and free Black individuals. This pervasive surveillance contributed to the overall atmosphere of fear and oppression that characterized the antebellum South, shaping social norms and reinforcing the **racial hierarchy** of the time.

Connection to Economic Prosperity

Patrols in the **antebellum South** played a pivotal role in shaping the economic prosperity of **plantation owners** through their enforcement of **labor control** and preservation of the existing **social order**. These patrols, comprised of white men often deputized to monitor enslaved populations, served as a fundamental tool in maintaining the profitability of the plantation economy. By ensuring the constant surveillance and regulation of enslaved individuals, these patrols deterred rebellious acts and minimized the risk of insurrection, thereby safeguarding the **economic investments** of plantation owners.

Furthermore, the presence of **slave patrols** instilled a sense of fear and submission among the **enslaved population**, thereby increasing the efficiency of labor extraction. The ability to discipline and punish enslaved individuals through the authority granted by these patrols not only secured the economic interests of plantation owners but also contributed to the overall expansion and profitability of the plantation system. As a result, the connection between slave patrols and economic prosperity in the antebellum South underscores the intertwined nature of labor control, social order, and **financial gain** in sustaining the plantation economy.

Resistance and Abolitionist Challenges

Resistance to the oppressive system maintained by **slave patrols** and the **plantation economy** in the antebellum South was met with formidable challenges posed by **abolitionist movements** seeking to dismantle the institution of slavery. Abolitionists, both black and white, employed various tactics to challenge the status quo. Black abolitionists like **Frederick Douglass** and **Harriet Tubman** played pivotal roles in advocating for the **immediate emancipation** of enslaved individuals and highlighting the brutalities of the system. They used their voices and actions to bring attention to the inhumane conditions faced by enslaved people and the need for their liberation.

White abolitionists, such as **William Lloyd Garrison** and **Angelina Grimké**, also played significant roles in the fight against slavery. They organized anti-slavery societies, published newspapers and pamphlets condemning slavery, and participated in **public lectures** and debates to sway public opinion against the institution. The abolitionist movement faced fierce opposition from pro-slavery advocates who sought to maintain the existing social and economic order. Despite these challenges, abolitionists remained steadfast in their commitment to achieving freedom and equality for all individuals, laying the groundwork for the eventual abolition of slavery in the United States.

Legacy of Slave Patrols in the South

Examining the historical ramifications of the **antebellum South** reveals a complex and vital legacy intertwined with the operations of law enforcement mechanisms. The legacy of **slave patrols** in the South transcends their abolition, leaving a lasting impact on American society. These patrols, originating in the early 18th century, were fundamental in maintaining the **institution of slavery** by controlling the movements and behaviors of enslaved individuals. Despite their dissolution after the **Civil War**, the practices and ideologies of slave patrols persisted, influencing the development of modern law enforcement agencies. The **racialized patterns** of surveillance and control established by these patrols laid the groundwork for **systemic racism** and discrimination that continue to plague the United States today.

Moreover, the tactics employed by slave patrols, such as arbitrary searches and brutal punishments, set a precedent for the **excessive use of force** and violence by law enforcement against **marginalized communities**. The deep-rooted prejudices and power dynamics embedded in the legacy of slave patrols underscore the ongoing struggles for justice and equality in contemporary American society. Understanding this legacy is vital in addressing the persistent inequities that stem from centuries of **oppressive policing practices**.

Conclusion

Ultimately, the institution of **slave patrols** played a significant role in the expansion of the **plantation economy** in the antebellum South. These patrols were instrumental in enforcing slave labor, maintaining social order, and contributing to **economic prosperity**.

Despite resistance and challenges from abolitionists, the legacy of slave patrols continues to impact the South to this day, serving as a reminder of the deep-rooted history of oppression and exploitation in the region.

CHAPTER 4: RESISTANCE AND REBELLION AGAINST SLAVE PATROLS

Slave Strategies for Evading Capture and Surveillance by Slave Patrols

Enslaved individuals employed **cunning deception** and strategic tactics to evade slave patrols. They utilized land knowledge, identifying hidden paths and safe havens. Communication networks with **coded language and signals** aided in information exchange. **Mastery of camouflage** and diversion tactics helped in slipping away unnoticed. By leveraging stealth and agility, they **outmaneuvered patrollers**. Seeking refuge in crucial spaces and using deception for autonomy were essential tactics. This blend of strategies empowered individuals seeking freedom. Understanding these methods sheds light on the resilience and ingenuity of those fighting oppression.

Key Takeaways

- Utilized knowledge of the land to identify hidden paths and safe havens.
- Employed sophisticated communication networks for exchanging information.
- Mastered camouflage by adapting to the natural environment.
- Strategically employed diversion tactics like creating disturbances.
- Leveraged stealth and agility to outmaneuver patrollers during pursuit.

Utilizing Knowledge of the Land

To evade capture by **slave patrols**, enslaved individuals strategically utilized their **knowledge of the land** to **navigate and outmaneuver** their pursuers. Enslaved people often possessed a deep understanding of the terrain surrounding their plantations, acquired through daily work routines, familial ties, and clandestine exploration. This intimate knowledge allowed them to identify **hidden paths**, **safe havens**, and areas with **limited visibility**, enabling quick escapes when faced with the threat of capture.

Plantations were typically situated in rural areas, characterized by **dense forests**, swamps, and intricate waterways. Enslaved individuals leveraged this environment to their advantage, utilizing **natural features** to throw off pursuit and conceal their movements. By exploiting their familiarity with the land, they could evade detection for extended periods, frustrating the efforts of slave patrols to track them down.

Furthermore, enslaved individuals often passed down information about the land through **oral traditions**, ensuring that subsequent generations could also benefit from this valuable knowledge. This intergenerational transfer of information solidified the effectiveness of utilizing the land as a strategic tool for evading capture by slave patrols.

Creating Communication Networks

Enslaved individuals employed **sophisticated communication networks** as a strategic method to **evade capture by slave patrols**, demonstrating remarkable ingenuity and resilience in maneuvering the oppressive systems of surveillance and control. These networks were pivotal in facilitating the exchange of information regarding patrol movements, safe routes, and potential hiding spots. By establishing covert methods of communication such as **coded language**, hidden messages, and **signal systems**, **enslaved individuals** were able to warn each other of impending danger and coordinate collective escape efforts.

One common strategy was the use of songs with hidden meanings that conveyed messages about **escape plans** or warned of **approaching patrols**. Additionally, individuals would utilize specific landmarks or natural elements to relay information discreetly, ensuring that essential details were shared without alerting slave owners or patrols. These communication networks not only enabled swift responses to immediate threats but also fostered a **sense of community** and solidarity among the enslaved population. Through these clandestine networks, individuals were able to resist the **constant surveillance** of slave patrols and assert a degree of autonomy in maneuvering their oppressive circumstances.

Mastering the Art of Camouflage

Employing intricate techniques of **blending into their surroundings**, enslaved individuals honed the skill of mastering the **art of camouflage** to evade detection by slave patrols. This strategic approach involved **adapting to the natural environment**, utilizing various techniques to conceal their presence. Enslaved individuals would often **mimic the behavior of animals**, moving quietly, and blending into foliage or shadows to avoid detection. By wearing **earth-toned clothing** and using **natural materials** to cover themselves, they decreased their visibility, making it harder for slave patrols to spot them.

Moreover, mastering the art of camouflage extended beyond physical appearance; it also encompassed behavioral aspects. Enslaved individuals learned to control their movements, avoid unnecessary noise, and remain vigilant of their surroundings. This **heightened sense of awareness** enabled them to anticipate potential threats and adapt their camouflage techniques accordingly. By combining both **physical and behavioral concealment strategies**, enslaved individuals increased their chances of evading capture and maneuvering through the perilous landscape of slavery.

Employing Diversion Tactics

In maneuvering the dangers posed by **slave patrols**, individuals in bondage strategically employed **diversion tactics** to redirect attention away from their true whereabouts. These tactics often involved **creating disturbances** or commotions in one area while **slipping away unnoticed** in another. For instance, slaves might intentionally start a **loud argument** or pretend to be engaged in a physical altercation to draw the focus of patrollers, allowing others to escape undetected. Additionally, some slaves would strategically **scatter belongings** or leave **false trails** to **mislead pursuers**, buying themselves essential time to distance themselves from immediate danger.

Diversion tactics required quick thinking, coordination, and a deep understanding of the environment to be effective. In densely wooded areas, slaves might imitate animal calls or rustling sounds to mask their movements, leading patrol members astray. By exploiting the element of surprise and utilizing distractions, individuals in bondage could outwit slave patrols and avoid capture, showcasing their resourcefulness and resilience in the face of constant surveillance and oppression.

Leveraging Stealth and Agility

Utilizing their surroundings to their advantage, individuals **maneuvering the perils** of **slave patrols** often leveraged **stealth** and agility as key tactics for evading capture. Stealth involved moving silently and remaining out of sight to avoid detection by patrollers. Slaves would camouflage themselves in the natural environment, using foliage or darkness to obscure their presence. This tactic allowed them to **navigate through dangerous territories undetected**, increasing their chances of escape.

Vital played a pivotal role in evading capture as well. Slaves relied on their **physical dexterity and quick reflexes** to **outmaneuver patrollers during pursuit**. By swiftly changing directions, climbing obstacles, or traversing challenging terrains, they could throw off their pursuers and create distance between themselves and the patrol. This agility enabled slaves to navigate through narrow passages or dense vegetation where patrollers struggled to follow, giving them a **strategic advantage in escaping capture**.

Seeking Refuge in Safe Spaces

To evade capture by **slave patrols**, seeking refuge in **safe spaces** emerged as an important strategy employed by individuals maneuvering the treacherous terrain of pursuit and capture. Safe spaces provided **temporary sanctuary** from the constant threat of being apprehended by slave patrols. These sanctuaries ranged from **hidden compartments** in homes to secret locations in the wilderness, offering moments of respite and safety for those fleeing captivity.

Individuals sought refuge in various places such as sympathetic neighbors' homes, **remote caves**, **thick forests**, or **secluded swamps** to avoid detection. These safe spaces allowed individuals to rest, regroup, and strategize their next steps without the immediate fear of being captured. Additionally, these locations often provided opportunities for individuals to connect with the **Underground Railroad network** or receive assistance from **abolitionist sympathizers**.

While seeking refuge in safe spaces was an important tactic in evading capture, individuals had to remain vigilant and cautious, as slave patrols actively searched these areas. Despite the risks involved, the utilization of safe spaces played a significant role in the survival and ultimate liberation of many individuals escaping the horrors of slavery.

Evading Pursuit through Deception

Deception emerged as a strategic method employed by individuals to outwit and evade pursuit by **slave patrols** in their relentless quest to capture **escaped slaves**. This tactic involved various forms of trickery, such as altering one's appearance, **creating false narratives** about one's identity or destination, and utilizing **coded language** to communicate covertly.

Escaped slaves would often dress as free individuals or even as members of the dominant society to blend in and avoid suspicion. They would **fabricate stories** about being on official business or heading to a nearby plantation, throwing off the patrols' scent. Additionally, slaves devised **secret signals** and phrases to signal danger or safety to one another, enabling them to navigate risky situations discreetly.

Deception not only allowed escaped slaves to outmaneuver slave patrols but also fostered a sense of empowerment and autonomy in a system designed to strip them of agency. This strategic use of **deception** highlights the ingenuity and resilience of individuals seeking freedom in the face of oppressive surveillance.

Conclusion

To sum up, the tactics utilized by slaves to **evade capture** and surveillance by **slave patrols** were vital for their survival and resistance.

One intriguing statistic to ponder is that based on historical records, slave patrols were accountable for apprehending and sending back thousands of escaped slaves each year.

This underscores the significance of the strategies employed by slaves to outsmart and outmaneuver their pursuers in order to **secure their freedom**.

Instances of Armed Resistance against Slave Patrols

Instances of armed resistance against slave patrols, such as Nat Turner's Rebellion and Gabriel Prosser's Uprising, showcased enslaved individuals' determination to challenge oppression. Denmark Vesey's Plot and Gullah Jack's Rebellion also highlighted the collective yearning for freedom and organized efforts to resist authority. The **Stono Rebellion** and **Louisiana Slave Revolt of 1811** further demonstrated discontent and defiance against the status quo. These events indicate the complexities of power dynamics and the lengths enslaved individuals were willing to go in their fight for liberation. Each uprising reveals a unique aspect of resistance history that sheds light on the relentless pursuit of freedom.

Key Takeaways

- Gullah Jack's Rebellion targeted slave patrols' authority in 1822.
- Organized resistance planned to challenge oppressive surveillance.
- Demonstrated leadership and organized defiance against patrols.
- Intended for a mass uprising to reflect collective desire for freedom.
- Foiled before execution, symbolizing resilience and impact of resistance.

Nat Turners Rebellion

Nat Turner's Rebellion in 1831 stands out as a significant event in American history due to its impact on the discourse surrounding slavery and resistance to slave patrols. Nat Turner, an **enslaved African American**, led one of the most well-known **slave rebellions** in **Southampton County, Virginia**. Turner, a preacher who believed he was **chosen by God** to lead his people to freedom, organized a group of enslaved individuals to revolt against their oppressors. The rebellion resulted in the deaths of around 60 white individuals before being suppressed by state and federal troops.

The aftermath of Nat Turner's Rebellion led to **harsher slave codes** and restrictions on enslaved people, further limiting their already minimal rights and freedoms. The event also sparked fear among **white slaveholders**, leading to increased surveillance and control over the enslaved population. Turner's bold and violent resistance highlighted the deep-rooted tensions and injustices of the **institution of slavery**, fueling debates on abolition and the treatment of enslaved individuals in the United States.

Gabriel Prossers Uprising

The uprising led by Gabriel Prosser in 1800, known as Gabriel Prosser's Uprising, was a significant event in American history that highlighted the resistance of **enslaved individuals** against the oppressive system of slavery.

Prosser, a literate blacksmith enslaved in Virginia, organized a **planned slave rebellion** involving thousands of enslaved individuals. The plan involved seizing the **state arsenal in Richmond** and overthrowing the **existing power structure**.

However, before the revolt could take place, it was betrayed by informants, leading to the capture of Prosser and his co-conspirators. This uprising showcased the deep discontent and **desire for freedom** among the enslaved population, as well as the lengths to which they were willing to go to secure their liberation.

Despite the failure of the rebellion, Gabriel Prosser's Uprising left a lasting impact on the enslaved community and served as a precursor to future **resistance efforts against the institution** of slavery.

Denmark Veseys Plot

In 1822, **Denmark Vesey**, a formerly enslaved man in **Charleston, South Carolina**, orchestrated a meticulously planned **slave rebellion** that aimed to challenge the **oppressive system of slavery** in the United States. Vesey, who had purchased his freedom after winning a local lottery, used his position as a **free man** to organize a revolt that involved thousands of enslaved individuals.

The plot involved seizing control of the city, arming themselves, and sailing to Haiti, a **free black republic**, for refuge. However, before the rebellion could take place, authorities were informed of the plan by other enslaved individuals, leading to the arrest of Vesey and his co-conspirators. The thwarting of Vesey's plot resulted in a wave of paranoia and fear among white slaveholders, leading to harsher restrictions on the enslaved population in the South.

Denmark Vesey's rebellion serves as a **poignant example of the lengths** to which enslaved individuals were willing to go to resist the brutal institution of slavery.

Stono Rebellion

The **Stono Rebellion**, also known as Cato's Conspiracy, marked one of the largest uprisings by **enslaved Africans** in the British mainland colonies prior to the American Revolution. This event took place on **September 9, 1739**, near the Stono River in South Carolina.

A group of approximately 20 enslaved Africans seized weapons and killed two shopkeepers, initiating a march south towards **Spanish Florida**, where they believed freedom awaited. As they marched, the group grew to nearly 100 individuals, burning houses and killing more colonists along the way.

The rebellion was eventually suppressed by the **local militia**, resulting in the deaths of many of the enslaved individuals involved. In the aftermath, **stricter laws** were enacted to control the movement and assembly of enslaved people, demonstrating the fear and backlash that such uprisings instilled in the white population.

The Stono Rebellion serves as a poignant example of the lengths to which enslaved Africans were willing to go to resist their **oppressive conditions**.

New York Conspiracy of 1741

Curiously, rarely do historical accounts fail to mention the **New York Conspiracy of 1741**, a significant event that sparked fear and hysteria throughout the colonial city.

The conspiracy unfolded in the midst of a tense climate of **economic hardship**, social unrest, and **racial tensions**. A series of fires in March and April of that year fueled suspicions of a planned **slave uprising**.

As investigations ensued, many enslaved Africans and poor whites were arrested and interrogated, leading to a wave of **sensational trials** and convictions. The testimonies of witnesses, often obtained through coercion and fear, implicated numerous individuals in a supposed plot to burn the city and overthrow the **colonial government**.

Ultimately, over 30 enslaved Africans and poor whites were executed, and many more were banished or sold into further enslavement. The New York Conspiracy of 1741 serves as a stark reminder of the pervasive climate of fear and control that characterized the dynamics between **enslaved individuals** and colonial authorities during this period.

Louisiana Slave Revolt of 1811

The **Louisiana Slave Revolt of 1811** stands out as a consequential event in American history, showcasing a significant challenge to the **system of slavery** and the authority of slaveholders in the region. This uprising, involving around 200 to 500 enslaved individuals, primarily from **sugar plantations** along the Mississippi River, aimed to **seize control of New Orleans**. The revolt began on January 8, 1811, led by **Charles Deslondes**, a mulatto slave driver who organized the rebellion with a group of trusted lieutenants.

The rebels marched towards the city, armed with firearms, clubs, and cane knives, displaying a coordinated effort that posed a serious threat to the existing power structures. Despite their determination, the **revolt was swiftly suppressed** by **local militia and federal troops**, resulting in many rebels being killed or captured. The brutal aftermath included **public executions**, with rebels' heads placed on pikes to serve as a warning to others.

The Louisiana Slave Revolt of 1811 highlights the deep-seated discontent among the enslaved population and the violent responses employed to maintain the institution of slavery in the United States.

Charles Deslondess Rebellion

Amidst the turbulent landscape of slavery in the **early 19th century**, **Charles Deslondes** orchestrated a daring rebellion that reverberated through the **sugar plantations** along the Mississippi River. Deslondes, a mixed-race slave driver on the **Andry sugar plantation** in Louisiana, led one of the **largest slave uprisings** in U.S. history in January 1811. Inspired by the Haitian Revolution and fueled by a desire for freedom, Deslondes organized a group of around 200 enslaved individuals to challenge the oppressive system they were bound to.

The rebellion started on January 8th, with Deslondes and his followers arming themselves with whatever weapons they could find, including **cane knives and firearms**. They marched from plantation to plantation, gaining more supporters and growing in number. The revolt was met with **brutal suppression by local militia** and federal troops. Deslondes was captured, and the **revolt was violently put down**. Deslondes was later executed, and many of the rebels were either killed in battle or captured and executed as a testimony to the deep yearning for freedom and dignity among the enslaved population of the time.

Gullah Jacks Rebellion

With a strategic and calculated approach, **Gullah Jack** orchestrated a **significant rebellion** against the **oppressive slave patrols** in the early 19th century. Gullah Jack, a trusted slave of his master, **Denmark Vesey**, in Charleston, South Carolina, played a **pivotal role** in planning and executing a rebellion that aimed to challenge the authority of slave patrols and seek freedom for enslaved individuals.

The rebellion, planned for July 1822, intended to incite a **mass uprising** of slaves in the region. Gullah Jack's leadership and organizational skills were evident in the detailed plans that involved coordinating efforts among various groups of enslaved individuals.

The rebellion, however, was foiled before it could be carried out, as authorities were alerted to the plans, resulting in the arrest of Gullah Jack and others involved. Despite its failure, Gullah Jack's rebellion remains a poignant example of **resistance against the oppression** of slave patrols and the collective yearning for freedom among the enslaved population.

Conclusion

To sum up, instances of **armed resistance** against slave patrols were significant events in the history of slavery in the United States. These rebellions, including Nat Turner's Rebellion, Gabriel Prosser's Uprising, and the Stono Rebellion, challenged the **oppressive system** of slavery and inspired others to resist.

The truth of these events highlights the determination of enslaved individuals to fight for their freedom and rights, despite the risks and hardships they faced.

Influence of Slave Resistance on Slave Patrol Tactics and Policies

Slave resistance during slavery era impacted slave patrol tactics and policies. Rebellions like Nat Turner's Rebellion prompted patrols to increase control measures. Enslaved individuals' sabotage challenged patrol authority. Policies evolved from informal to systematic, becoming more oppressive. **Fugitive Slave Acts** expanded patrols' jurisdiction. **Slave resistance** disrupted plantation operations, exposing the brutality of slavery. This resistance shaped **antebellum society dynamics**.

Key Takeaways

- Slave resistance prompted harsher patrol tactics and policies
- Acts of rebellion and sabotage led to increased surveillance
- Escapes forced patrols to intensify their efforts
- Resistance challenged the effectiveness of patrol control
- Slave defiance shaped the evolution of patrol strategies and laws

Forms of Slave Resistance

Slave resistance during the era of slavery in the United States encompassed a variety of forms, ranging from subtle acts of defiance to **organized rebellions**. One significant form of resistance was **day-to-day acts of defiance**, such as **feigning illness**, breaking tools, or working slowly. These actions were ways for slaves to exert some level of control and resistance within the oppressive system they were subjected to.

Another form of resistance was **running away**, either temporarily to visit family on nearby plantations or permanently in search of freedom in the North or Canada via the **Underground Railroad**.

Moreover, organized rebellions, such as Nat Turner's Rebellion in 1831 and the **Stono Rebellion** in 1739, were vital instances of slave resistance that challenged the institution of slavery more directly. These rebellions were often met with severe consequences, including harsher treatment of all slaves and more stringent control measures.

Role of Slave Patrols

How did the establishment and operation of **slave patrols** influence the dynamics of power and control within the institution of slavery in the United States?

Slave patrols played a significant role in maintaining the oppressive system of slavery by **enforcing discipline** and preventing slave rebellions. These patrols, typically composed of white men from the local community, were empowered to monitor the movements of enslaved individuals, **search for runaway slaves**, and suppress any signs of resistance or defiance.

The mere presence of slave patrols instilled fear among the enslaved population, reminding them of the consequences of disobedience. Additionally, the patrols served as a visible symbol of **white dominance** and authority over Black individuals, reinforcing the **racial hierarchy** ingrained in the fabric of **American society**.

Tactics Employed by Enslaved Individuals

Enslaved individuals strategically employed a variety of **covert tactics** to resist the oppressive control imposed upon them by slave patrols and slave owners. These tactics were born out of a deep-seated desire for freedom and autonomy in the face of extreme adversity. One common tactic was **feigning illness** or injury to avoid work or **gain temporary respite** from the **harsh conditions of slavery**. By appearing weak or incapacitated, enslaved individuals could subvert the demands of their oppressors and assert a degree of control over their own bodies and labor.

Another tactic employed by enslaved individuals was the **manipulation of their work pace** and output. By deliberately working slowly or making subtle errors, they could undermine the efficiency and profitability of their labor, thereby resisting the dehumanizing effects of being treated as mere commodities. Additionally, some enslaved individuals engaged in **acts of sabotage**, such as damaging tools or crops, as a form of covert resistance against the exploitative system of slavery. These tactics, though seemingly small in scale, were **powerful acts of defiance** that **challenged the authority** of slave patrols and plantation owners.

Evolution of Slave Patrol Policies

The development of policies governing **slave patrols** underwent a complex evolution shaped by **societal norms**, **economic interests**, and **power dynamics** within the institution of slavery. Initially, slave patrol policies were informally structured, with white men in the Southern colonies forming groups to monitor and control enslaved populations.

As slavery became more entrenched in the economic fabric of the Southern states, formal legislation was enacted to regulate and empower these patrols. Laws such as the **Slave Codes** granted extensive authority to slave patrollers, allowing them to stop, search, and punish enslaved individuals at will.

Over time, these policies evolved to become more systematic and oppressive. Slave patrols were given broader jurisdiction, and their tactics became increasingly **violent and dehumanizing**. The **Fugitive Slave Acts** further empowered patrols, enabling them to pursue escaped slaves across state lines.

The evolution of slave patrol policies mirrored the deepening divide between enslaved individuals seeking freedom and the slaveholders determined to maintain control, culminating in a **repressive system** that perpetuated the institution of slavery.

Impact on Antebellum Society

The evolution of slave patrol policies during the **antebellum period** deeply influenced the **societal structure** and dynamics of the time, revealing intricate intersections between power, resistance, and control. In antebellum society, where slavery was a cornerstone of the economy and social order, **slave patrols** played a significant role in maintaining the institution by exerting control over enslaved individuals. The presence of these patrols instilled fear among the enslaved population, reinforcing the power dynamics that upheld the system of slavery.

Furthermore, the **resistance shown** by enslaved individuals in response to these patrols directly challenged the authority of **slave owners** and the state. Acts of rebellion, escape, and sabotage not only disrupted the **daily operations** of plantations but also highlighted the inherent cruelty and inhumanity of the slave system. This resistance, coupled with the increasingly stringent tactics employed by slave patrols, contributed to **heightened tensions** within antebellum society, exposing the fragility of a system built on oppression and exploitation. The impact of **slave resistance** on slave patrol policies reverberated throughout antebellum society, shaping perceptions of power, race, and control.

Conclusion

To sum up, the **resistance of enslaved individuals** played a significant role in shaping the tactics and policies of **slave patrols**. The constant struggle between enslaved individuals and slave patrols led to the evolution of increasingly oppressive measures.

This dynamic relationship between resistance and control created a society where **fear and violence** were pervasive, painting a dark and haunting picture of the antebellum South.

CHAPTER 5: EVOLUTION OF SLAVE PATROLS POST-EMANCIPATION

Transition of Slave Patrols to Law Enforcement Agencies

The move from **slave patrols** to **modern law enforcement agencies** marks a significant shift in policing's structure and function. This transformation reflects historical complexities that still influence societal norms, practices, and disparities today. Understanding this evolution is vital in examining the origins of policing and its impact on racial inequalities. The historical legacy of slave patrols continues to shape modern police forces, raising concerns about **systemic racism**, excessive force, and biased practices. Exploring this change sheds light on the intricate relationship between past injustices and **current policing challenges**.

Key Takeaways

- Slave patrols evolved into centralized law enforcement agencies.
- Changes in structure, training, and procedures occurred.
- Aim shifted towards enhancing accountability and fairness.
- Reflected broader societal shifts towards rule of law.
- Historical roots intertwined with perpetuation of racial inequalities.

Evolution into Law Enforcement

The development of **slave patrols** into official **law enforcement agencies** in the United States marked a significant change in the structure and function of policing within American society. As the nation progressed beyond the era of slavery, the need for a more organized and **centralized system of law enforcement** became apparent. This shift involved the establishment of official police forces tasked with maintaining **public order**, enforcing laws, and protecting citizens.

The evolution into law enforcement brought about changes in training, procedures, and the overall approach to maintaining public safety. Officers began to be trained in standardized protocols, legal frameworks, and **community policing strategies**. The move towards a more **professionalized and regulated system** of law enforcement aimed to enhance accountability and ensure the fair treatment of all individuals under the law.

Moreover, the development into formal law enforcement agencies reflected **broader societal shifts** towards the rule of law and the protection of individual rights. This transformation laid the foundation for **modern policing practices** and the intricate relationship between law enforcement agencies and the communities they serve.

Impact on Racial Inequalities

The assimilation of **former slave patrols** into official law enforcement agencies directly intertwined the historical roots of policing in the United States with the perpetuation of **racial inequalities**. This shift laid the foundation for **systemic discrimination** and bias in law enforcement practices, which continue to impact racial minorities today. The legacy of slave patrols, which were tasked with controlling and oppressing Black individuals, manifested in the form of **racial profiling**, **excessive use of force**, and **unequal treatment** towards people of color within the criminal justice system.

The inherent racial biases ingrained in the early practices of policing have evolved over time but remain prevalent in modern law enforcement agencies. Studies have shown that African Americans and other minority groups are disproportionately targeted for stops, arrests, and harsher sentencing compared to their white counterparts. This unequal treatment not only perpetuates **racial disparities** in the criminal justice system but also erodes trust between law enforcement and communities of color, hindering efforts to foster **positive relationships** and guarantee equitable protection for all citizens.

Modern Police Forces Today

Amidst ongoing debates surrounding **policing practices** and calls for reform, the structure and functions of **modern police forces** today continue to reflect the **historical legacy** of slave patrols in the United States. The origins of modern law enforcement agencies can be traced back to the slave patrols of the 18th and 19th centuries, which were tasked with controlling and suppressing enslaved populations. This historical connection has had a lasting impact on the relationship between law enforcement and **marginalized communities**.

Today, modern police forces often face criticism for perpetuating **systemic issues** such as **racial profiling**, **excessive use of force**, and **discriminatory practices**. The militarization of police departments, surveillance technologies, and the **lack of accountability** mechanisms further exacerbate these concerns. The legacy of slave patrols has influenced not only the structure and tactics of policing but also the underlying attitudes and biases that shape interactions between law enforcement officers and the communities they serve.

Efforts to reform policing practices and build trust between police and communities must acknowledge this historical legacy and work towards addressing the systemic issues that continue to perpetuate inequalities in modern law enforcement agencies.

Addressing Systemic Racism

Building upon the historical legacy of slave patrols influencing modern law enforcement agencies, a critical aspect that demands thorough attention is addressing **systemic racism** within policing practices today. Systemic racism in policing refers to the institutionalized policies and practices within law enforcement that perpetuates **racial discrimination and inequality**. This issue manifests in various forms, including **racial profiling**, **excessive use of force** against minorities, and **disparities in the treatment** of individuals based on their race or ethnicity.

Addressing systemic racism requires a holistic approach that involves acknowledging the existence of racial bias, implementing **anti-racism training for officers**, promoting diversity within police departments, and holding law enforcement accountable for discriminatory behavior. Additionally, **community engagement and collaboration** with organizations advocating for racial justice play an essential role in reforming policing practices and building trust between law enforcement and marginalized communities.

Conclusion

To sum up, the **evolution of slave patrols** to contemporary law enforcement agencies has had a **lasting impact** on racial inequalities in society.

One noteworthy statistic to note is that a study by the ACLU found that black people are three times more likely to be killed by police than white people.

This underscores the persistent issues of **systemic racism** within the criminal justice system that must be tackled for true equality to be attained.

Continuation of Racially Biased Policing Practices after Slave Patrols

Continuing the historical legacy of **systemic discrimination**, **racially biased policing practices** endure post-slave patrols. From Jim Crow segregation to the War on Drugs, marginalized communities face disproportionate scrutiny. The **Broken Windows theory** often leads to over-policing in minority neighborhoods. **Militarization of police** escalates tensions, eroding trust. Disproportionate use of force on Black and Hispanic individuals highlights the need for reforms. **Mass incarceration policies** target minorities, affecting families and reintegration post-release. Bias in **stop-and-frisk perpetuates racial profiling**, straining police-community relations. Addressing these challenges requires transparency, accountability, and cultural competency in law enforcement. Understanding these issues better equips us to advocate for change.

Key Takeaways

- Transition from slave patrols to law enforcement agencies
- Preservation of racial biases in policing practices
- Enforcement of segregation and discriminatory laws
- Continuation of oppressive tactics in marginalized communities
- Legacy of systemic racism influencing modern policing

Origins of Racial Profiling

The practice of **racial profiling** traces its origins back to historical instances of **discriminatory targeting** based on perceived characteristics such as race, ethnicity, or nationality. Throughout history, marginalized communities have been disproportionately subjected to **unjust scrutiny** and surveillance by law enforcement agencies. Racial profiling perpetuates **systemic inequality** and undermines the principles of justice and equality.

Rooted in prejudice and stereotypes, racial profiling has been used to justify the unjust treatment of individuals solely based on their appearance or background. This discriminatory practice not only violates **civil liberties** but also erodes trust between law enforcement and the communities they serve.

Policing in Jim Crow Era

Policing practices during the **Jim Crow Era** were characterized by **systemic discrimination** and segregation enforced by laws and policies that perpetuated **racial inequality**. In this period of American history, law enforcement played a pivotal role in upholding the oppressive Jim Crow laws that enforced **racial segregation** and **white supremacy**. Police officers were often complicit in maintaining the racial hierarchy by actively discriminating against African Americans through **biased policing practices**. African Americans faced harassment, violence, and unjust treatment at the hands of law enforcement, further entrenching racial divides in society.

During the Jim Crow Era, police departments were mainly white and operated under the belief in the inherent superiority of white individuals over people of color. This mindset translated into discriminatory practices such as **racial profiling**, excessive use of force, and unequal application of the law based on race. The legacy of racially biased policing during this era continues to impact communities of color today, highlighting the enduring effects of **historical injustices** on modern law enforcement practices.

War on Drugs Impact

Amidst the ongoing debate surrounding law enforcement practices in the United States, the impact of the **War on Drugs** remains a contentious issue with far-reaching implications for communities of color. Initiated in the 1970s, the War on Drugs disproportionately targeted **minority communities**, leading to increased arrests, convictions, and incarceration rates among people of color. This approach, fueled by policies such as **mandatory minimum sentencing** and the prioritization of drug law enforcement, has perpetuated **systemic racial disparities** within the criminal justice system.

Communities of color have borne the brunt of aggressive policing tactics, including **stop-and-frisk policies** and no-knock warrants, which have exacerbated tensions between law enforcement and marginalized groups. The **collateral consequences** of these practices extend beyond individuals to entire communities, creating cycles of poverty, trauma, and distrust in the criminal justice system.

Moreover, the War on Drugs has failed to address the root causes of **substance abuse and addiction**, instead emphasizing **punitive measures** over rehabilitation and support. As efforts to reform **drug policies** gain momentum, it is essential to acknowledge and rectify the discriminatory impact of past strategies on communities of color.

Broken Windows Policing

Given the significant impact on communities and law enforcement practices, **Broken Windows Policing** has been a subject of scrutiny and debate in recent years. This policing strategy, introduced by **Wilson and Kelling** in 1982, suggests that **visible signs of disorder** and neglect in neighborhoods can create an environment conducive to crime. Proponents argue that by addressing minor infractions like vandalism and public intoxication, more serious crimes can be prevented. However, critics highlight the potential for **racial profiling** and the disproportionate targeting of minority communities under this approach.

Critics argue that Broken Windows Policing can exacerbate existing racial biases within law enforcement, leading to the **over-policing of minority neighborhoods** and the **criminalization of poverty**. Studies have shown that communities of color are often subjected to more intense policing under this strategy, resulting in **higher rates of arrest** and incarceration for minor offenses. As a result, calls for reforming or abolishing Broken Windows Policing have gained traction in recent years, with advocates pushing for alternative approaches that prioritize **community engagement** and address the underlying causes of crime.

Militarization of Police

The escalation of **militarization** within law enforcement agencies has raised concerns regarding the **erosion of community trust** and the potential reinforcement of **systemic racial biases** in policing practices. The increasing use of **military equipment** and tactics by police forces can create an environment of fear and intimidation, especially in communities of color. The adoption of military-style gear, such as armored vehicles and camouflage uniforms, can send a message of aggression rather than one of **community service** and protection.

Moreover, the militarization of police can lead to a mindset more focused on treating civilians as **potential enemies** rather than as individuals to serve and protect. This shift in mentality can exacerbate tensions between law enforcement and the communities they are meant to serve, further **widening the gap** of trust and understanding.

Efforts to address the militarization of police should involve reevaluating the necessity of such equipment and tactics in **civilian policing contexts**. Building strong community relationships based on transparency, accountability, and mutual respect is essential to counteracting the negative impacts of militarization and fostering safer and more inclusive communities.

Disproportionate Use of Force

The issue of **extensive use of force** within law enforcement is a critical concern that demands careful examination and proactive measures to address **systemic disparities** in policing practices. Extensive use of force refers to the unequal application of force by law enforcement officers, often targeting **marginalized communities** based on race, ethnicity, or socio-economic status. This practice not only violates the principles of justice and equality but also erodes trust between law enforcement agencies and the communities they serve.

Studies have shown that communities of color are disproportionately affected by **police violence**, with Black and Hispanic individuals being more likely to experience the inappropriate use of force compared to their white counterparts. Factors such as **implicit bias**, **lack of accountability**, and inadequate training can contribute to these disparities.

Addressing the issue of extensive use of force requires thorough reforms that prioritize de-escalation tactics, **community policing** strategies, and enhanced officer training on **cultural competency** and implicit bias, as well as strict accountability measures for officers who engage in **excessive force**. By implementing these changes, law enforcement agencies can work towards building trust, promoting fairness, and ensuring the safety of all individuals within the communities they serve.

Mass Incarceration Policies

With the rise of **mass incarceration** policies in the United States, there has been a profound impact on **marginalized communities**, highlighting **systemic issues** within the criminal justice system. These policies have led to a disproportionately high number of Black and Hispanic individuals being incarcerated compared to their white counterparts. The **War on Drugs** in the 1980s and 1990s, for example, resulted in **harsh sentencing laws** that targeted **minority communities**, contributing to the current crisis of mass incarceration.

Mass incarceration not only affects individuals behind bars but also has far-reaching consequences for families and communities. Children of incarcerated parents, mainly from minority backgrounds, face numerous challenges, including **financial instability** and limited access to educational and social support systems. Additionally, the cycle of incarceration perpetuates as individuals released from prison encounter difficulties in reintegrating into society due to stigma and lack of opportunities.

To address the systemic inequalities perpetuated by mass incarceration, policymakers must reevaluate sentencing laws, invest in **community-based rehabilitation programs**, and prioritize prevention and intervention strategies over **punitive measures**. Only through thorough reform can the criminal justice system begin to rectify the injustices inflicted on marginalized communities.

Bias in Stop-and-Frisk

Continuing the examination of **systemic injustices** in the criminal justice system, the practice of **stop-and-frisk** has come under scrutiny for its perpetuation of bias and **racial profiling**. Stop-and-frisk policies empower law enforcement officers to detain, question, and search individuals based on mere suspicion of criminal activity, often leading to the targeting of **minority communities**. Studies have consistently shown that **people of color**, particularly Black and Latino individuals, are disproportionately subjected to these searches compared to their white counterparts.

The bias in stop-and-frisk not only undermines trust between law enforcement and the community but also perpetuates stereotypes and prejudices. Critics argue that these practices do little to enhance **public safety** and instead contribute to the **criminalization of communities** of color. The over-policing and aggressive tactics associated with stop-and-frisk can have long-lasting negative consequences on individuals' lives, leading to feelings of harassment, fear, and alienation. Addressing the biases embedded in stop-and-frisk policies is essential in promoting **fair and equitable policing practices**.

Community Policing Challenges

What are the key obstacles faced by law enforcement agencies in effectively implementing **community policing** strategies to foster trust and collaboration within diverse communities?

Community policing, aimed at building partnerships and proactive problem-solving, faces several challenges in its implementation. One obstacle is the **historical legacy of mistrust** between law enforcement and marginalized communities, stemming from past discriminatory practices. Overcoming this deep-rooted distrust requires significant efforts in **transparency, accountability**, and **cultural competency training** for officers.

Additionally, resource constraints and **competing priorities** within police departments can hinder the full adoption of community policing approaches. **Limited funding** for community engagement programs or insufficient staffing levels may impede the establishment of meaningful relationships with diverse community members.

Moreover, **resistance to change** within law enforcement **organizational culture** can pose a barrier to the successful implementation of community policing strategies. Traditional **top-down hierarchical structures** may impede officers' autonomy and discretion in engaging with communities in a collaborative manner.

Addressing these challenges requires an all-encompassing approach that includes **cultural sensitivity training**, adequate resource allocation, and **leadership commitment** to promoting community policing as a cornerstone of modern law enforcement practices. By actively overcoming these obstacles, law enforcement agencies can work towards fostering trust, improving relationships, and enhancing public safety within diverse communities.

Conclusion

In examining the continuation of **racially biased policing practices** from the slave patrols to modern law enforcement, it is evident that **systemic racism** remains deeply ingrained within the criminal justice system.

The historical roots of racial profiling, coupled with policies such as the **War on Drugs** and **Broken Windows policing**, have disproportionately affected communities of color.

To address these issues, there must be a reevaluation of policing strategies and a commitment to fostering trust and accountability within communities.

Legacy of Slave Patrols in Modern Law Enforcement

The significance of **slave patrols** in modern law enforcement is profound. Dating back to the 1700s, these patrols instilled **surveillance, violence, and control** tactics still seen today. Their **hierarchical structure** and **'us versus them' mentality** endure in policing culture, influencing behaviors. The use of violence by patrols echoes in aggressive modern tactics, perpetuating distrust among communities of color. **Racial bias** persists, leading to disparities in treatment and systemic injustices. Understanding this historical linkage is vital for grasping current law enforcement dynamics and challenges. The impact of slave patrols lingers, shaping modern policing practices and attitudes.

Key Takeaways

- Slave patrols influenced modern policing culture and practices.
- Hierarchical structures in law enforcement trace back to control dynamics of slave patrols.
- Historical use of violence by slave patrols impacts aggressive tactics in modern law enforcement.
- Racial bias persists, seen in disproportionate targeting of people of color.
- Legacy of discriminatory practices deepens mistrust between police and marginalized communities.

Historical Roots of Modern Policing

In tracing the historical roots of modern policing, it becomes evident that the evolution of law enforcement in society is intertwined with the legacy of **slave patrols** in the United States. Slave patrols were established in the southern U.S. colonies during the 1700s to control enslaved populations, prevent revolts, and maintain the **institution of slavery**. These patrols were the precursors to **modern police forces**, shaping the foundation of **law enforcement practices** in the country.

Slave patrols were responsible for monitoring the movements of enslaved individuals, **enforcing curfews**, and punishing those who attempted to escape or violate plantation rules. The tactics and strategies employed by these patrols, such as **surveillance, intimidation, and violence**, laid the groundwork for the policing methods used by law enforcement agencies today.

The legacy of slave patrols in modern policing extends beyond their operational practices. It includes the perpetuation of **racial biases**, unequal treatment, and **systemic discrimination** within law enforcement institutions. Understanding this historical connection is vital for comprehending the complexities of contemporary law enforcement and the ongoing struggles for justice and equality in society.

Influence on Law Enforcement Culture

Embedded within the fabric of law enforcement culture in the United States is the **enduring influence** of **slave patrols**, shaping the attitudes, behaviors, and practices of modern police forces. The historical roots of policing through slave patrols have left a lasting impact on law enforcement culture.

The **hierarchical structure**, where power and authority are concentrated at the top, can be traced back to the control dynamics of slave patrols. Additionally, the **'us versus them' mentality** ingrained in slave patrols, where the enslaved population was seen as a threat to be controlled, has permeated modern police attitudes towards **marginalized communities**.

Furthermore, the use of **violence and coercion** as tools of control by slave patrols has influenced the aggressive tactics sometimes employed by law enforcement today. This cultural legacy has contributed to the **lack of trust** and cooperation between law enforcement and communities of color, perpetuating tensions and hindering effective policing strategies.

Continuation of Racial Bias

The persistence of **racial bias** within modern **law enforcement agencies** underscores a deep-rooted issue that continues to impact interactions between police and communities of color. Despite efforts to promote diversity and **cultural sensitivity**, studies show that people of color are disproportionately targeted for stops, searches, and the use of force compared to their white counterparts. This **systemic bias** is evident in various aspects of policing, including arrest rates, **sentencing disparities**, and the treatment of minority individuals in mostly white neighborhoods.

Historical injustices, such as the enforcement of discriminatory laws and the perpetuation of stereotypes, have contributed to the continuation of racial bias within law enforcement. **Implicit biases** held by individual officers, as well as institutional practices that disproportionately affect communities of color, further exacerbate the issue. Addressing racial bias in policing requires a multifaceted approach that includes cultural competency training, community engagement, and **accountability measures** to make sure fair and **equitable treatment** for all individuals, regardless of their race or ethnicity.

Impact on Community Relations

A critical examination of the impact on community relations reveals the essential dynamics at play between law enforcement agencies and the diverse communities they serve. The historical roots of **slave patrols** have left a lasting imprint, fostering **mistrust and unease** among marginalized communities towards law enforcement. The legacy of discriminatory practices, **racial profiling**, and **excessive use of force** has deepened the divide between police forces and the people they are meant to protect.

These tensions manifest in various ways, including **strained interactions**, **lack of transparency**, and challenges in communication. Communities of color often view law enforcement with skepticism, fearing unjust treatment or violence. This breakdown in trust hinders effective policing efforts, as cooperation and collaboration are essential for ensuring public safety.

To improve community relations, proactive measures such as community policing initiatives, **cultural sensitivity training**, and **accountability mechanisms** are vital. Building bridges through dialogue, empathy, and mutual respect can help repair the fractured relationship between law enforcement and the communities they serve. By acknowledging the historical legacy of slave patrols and actively working towards reconciliation, law enforcement agencies can begin to rebuild trust and foster **positive community relationships**.

Role in Policing Practices Today

In contemporary law enforcement practices, the historical legacy of **slave patrols** continues to influence the dynamics between police forces and the communities they serve. The origins of policing in the United States, rooted in the slave patrols of the 18th and 19th centuries, have left a lasting impact on **modern policing strategies**. The emphasis on surveillance, control, and the use of force that characterized slave patrols still resonates in current policing practices, affecting interactions between law enforcement officers and **marginalized communities**.

This historical legacy has perpetuated systemic issues such as **racial profiling**, **unequal treatment**, and **distrust between law enforcement** and minority groups. The **deep-rooted biases** and power dynamics established during the era of slave patrols persist today, shaping the ways in which police approach their roles in society. As a result, communities of color often experience disproportionate levels of surveillance and enforcement, contributing to ongoing tensions and challenges in building **positive relationships** between police departments and the communities they are meant to protect and serve.

Connection to Use of Force

The **historical roots** of policing in the United States, particularly from the **era of slave patrols**, have greatly influenced the **contemporary use of force** by law enforcement agencies. The legacy of slave patrols, which were tasked with controlling enslaved populations through violent and coercive means, has contributed to a **culture within law enforcement** that sometimes prioritizes force over **de-escalation techniques**. This historical connection has manifested in modern law enforcement practices, where the use of force is often **disproportionately directed towards marginalized communities**, particularly Black and Brown individuals.

The utilization of force by law enforcement is a complex issue influenced by a variety of factors, including training, policies, and the **socio-political context** in which policing operates. However, the **historical precedent** set by slave patrols has undeniably shaped the way in which force is wielded by some officers today. To address this issue effectively, it is important to acknowledge and confront this historical connection, and work towards implementing reforms that prioritize the protection and respect of all individuals in society.

Challenges to Reform Efforts

Persistent institutional resistance poses significant obstacles to reform efforts aimed at addressing the historical legacy of slave patrols in modern law enforcement practices. This resistance often stems from a variety of factors, including **deeply ingrained cultural norms** within law enforcement agencies, **fear of change** among personnel, and **political challenges** that hinder meaningful reform. Law enforcement institutions are typically resistant to **external oversight and accountability measures**, which can impede efforts to address systemic issues rooted in historical practices like slave patrols.

Moreover, the strong **bond of loyalty and solidarity** among law enforcement officers can create a **culture of protectionism**, making it difficult to challenge and change established norms and practices. The **hierarchical structure** of many law enforcement agencies also contributes to the resistance against reform, as **dissenting voices** may face backlash or ostracization within the organization.

Additionally, the influence of **police unions** and their resistance to changes in policies and practices further complicates reform efforts. These unions often wield significant power in negotiating labor contracts and shaping departmental policies, which can hinder attempts to implement meaningful reforms aimed at addressing the historical legacy of slave patrols.

Addressing Systemic Inequities

Amidst the complexities of modern law enforcement practices, addressing **systemic inequities** requires a thorough and multi-faceted approach that explores **historical roots** and current manifestations of injustice. Systemic inequities in law enforcement are deeply ingrained, stemming from historical practices like slave patrols that have evolved into biases and discriminatory actions within the criminal justice system.

To address these inequities effectively, it is essential to implement reforms that focus on accountability, transparency, and community engagement. This can involve measures such as implementing **implicit bias training** for officers, **diversifying police forces** to better represent the communities they serve, and establishing **oversight mechanisms** to monitor and address discriminatory practices.

Additionally, investing in community programs that support **marginalized populations**, such as mental health services, substance abuse treatment, and affordable housing, can help address the underlying issues that contribute to **disparities in law enforcement interactions**.

Conclusion

The legacy of **slave patrols** in modern law enforcement is deeply ingrained in the culture and practices of policing. This historical influence continues to perpetuate **racial bias** and hinder efforts to build trust with communities.

The connection to use of force and **systemic inequities** presents significant challenges to reform. The impact of these roots on contemporary policing cannot be overstated, highlighting the urgent need for thorough and transformative change in law enforcement practices.

CHAPTER 6: CASE STUDIES AND EXAMPLES

Specific Instances of Slave Patrol Operations and Their Impacts

Slave patrol operations in Colonial America included **night watches** and militias enforcing curfews to restrain enslaved individuals. Their surveillance methods used armed patrols, informants, and **pass systems** to maintain control, instilling fear and anxiety. Resistance and escapes showcased enslaved individuals' courage and drive for freedom. These oppressive tactics resulted in profound **psychological and physical trauma**, impacting generations. This systemic exploitation perpetuated poverty and mental health challenges in Black communities, influencing **modern policing practices**. A deeper exploration reveals the enduring legacy of slave patrols on societal structures.

Key Takeaways

- Slave patrols operated under colonial government authority with broad powers.
- Patrollers composed of white men from militias, enforcing control over enslaved populations.
- Surveillance methods included night watches, curfews, and pass systems.
- Impact on enslaved individuals led to stress, anxiety, and limited autonomy.
- Legacy of oppression perpetuated systemic exploitation, marginalization, and mental health challenges in Black communities.

Early Slave Patrols in Colonial America

During the early years of colonial America, the establishment of **slave patrols** emerged as a systematic method of controlling and surveilling enslaved populations. These patrols were typically composed of **white men**, often drawn from the **local militias** or volunteer groups, tasked with maintaining order and preventing any **potential uprisings** or escapes among the enslaved individuals.

The first recorded slave patrol was established in the **Carolina colonies** in the early 1700s, with other Southern states quickly following suit.

Slave patrols operated under the authority of colonial governments and were granted **wide-ranging powers** to stop, question, search, and even use violence against enslaved individuals deemed to be behaving in a suspicious or rebellious manner. The patrols also served as a means of reinforcing the **racial hierarchy** and ensuring the dominance of the white population over their enslaved counterparts.

This system of surveillance and control not only instilled fear among the enslaved communities but also perpetuated the **dehumanization** and subjugation of African Americans in colonial society.

Night Watches and Militia Involvement

Night watches and the involvement of **militias** played a pivotal role in the implementation and enforcement of **slave patrols** in colonial America. **Night watches** were established in various colonies to maintain order, protect against **potential uprisings**, and prevent enslaved individuals from escaping. These watches often consisted of **white men** who patrolled the streets at night, checking for any signs of unrest among the enslaved population.

Militias, on the other hand, were more formally organized groups that were called upon to assist in slave patrols when needed. These militias were comprised of able-bodied white men who were responsible for not only quelling slave rebellions but also for capturing and returning runaway slaves to their owners. The involvement of militias added a layer of intimidation and force to the slave patrols, reinforcing the **power dynamics** of the time.

Methods of Surveillance and Control

The utilization of **informants within local communities** emerged as a strategic method employed by slave patrols to **enhance surveillance and control** over enslaved populations in colonial America. These informants often consisted of **white community members** who were incentivized to report any suspicious activities or potential escape plans among the enslaved individuals.

Slave patrols also utilized a system of **regular patrols**, where armed groups would move throughout plantations and rural areas, **instilling fear** and asserting their presence. Additionally, slave patrols implemented **curfews and pass systems**, restricting the movement of enslaved individuals and requiring them to carry passes when off the plantation.

This constant monitoring and restriction of movement aimed to prevent uprisings and escape attempts, reinforcing the dominance of slaveholders and the oppressive nature of the institution of slavery. The combination of these surveillance methods created an environment of **constant scrutiny and control**, further dehumanizing and subjugating the enslaved population.

Impact on Enslaved Individuals Daily Lives

The pervasive atmosphere of **surveillance and control** maintained by **slave patrols** infiltrated every aspect of enslaved individuals' daily existence, shaping their experiences and limiting their autonomy in profound ways. Enslaved individuals lived under constant fear of being apprehended by these patrols, leading to **heightened levels of stress** and anxiety. The mere presence of patrollers instilled a sense of **powerlessness and vulnerability** among the enslaved population, affecting their mental and emotional well-being.

Moreover, the **stringent regulations** imposed by slave patrols restricted the movements and activities of enslaved individuals. They faced limitations on where they could go, who they could interact with, and what tasks they could perform. This control extended to their family life, as **separations and disruptions** caused by patrols were common occurrences. The oppressive nature of these restrictions stripped enslaved individuals of basic human freedoms and perpetuated a **cycle of dehumanization**.

In essence, the impact of slave patrols on enslaved individuals' daily lives was pervasive and debilitating, fostering an environment of constant surveillance, control, and restriction that left **lasting scars on the psyche** of those subjected to such oppression.

Resistance and Escapes from Patrols

Amidst the **pervasive atmosphere of surveillance** and control imposed by slave patrols, instances of resistance and escapes emerged as **acts of defiance and liberation** among the enslaved population.

Enslaved individuals, despite facing severe consequences if caught, displayed **remarkable courage and resourcefulness** in their efforts to resist the authority of slave patrols. Some chose to run away, **seeking freedom in the face** of great danger, while others engaged in **subtle acts of rebellion** to undermine the effectiveness of patrol efforts. Resistance took various forms, from sabotage and feigned ignorance to open confrontations and physical altercations.

Escapes were often **meticulously planned**, with individuals relying on networks of assistance from free Black communities, sympathetic white allies, and Indigenous tribes. These acts of resistance and escapes not only posed challenges to the authority of slave patrols but also served as symbols of resilience and the **unyielding human spirit** in the pursuit of freedom and dignity.

Psychological and Physical Trauma

As a result of the brutal and dehumanizing conditions enforced by **slave patrols**, the enslaved population endured profound **psychological and physical trauma** that left lasting scars on their well-being and sense of self. The constant fear of being hunted, captured, and subjected to violence by slave patrols instilled a deep sense of **anxiety and helplessness** among the enslaved individuals. The psychological impact of living under such oppressive conditions manifested in various forms, including anxiety disorders, depression, and **post-traumatic stress symptoms** that persisted long after their physical freedom was attained.

Moreover, the physical trauma inflicted by slave patrols through beatings, torture, and other forms of punishment resulted in **severe injuries and disabilities** for many enslaved individuals. The **lack of proper medical care** and the harsh living conditions further exacerbated their suffering, leading to **long-term health complications** and chronic pain. These experiences of psychological and physical trauma not only affected the individual enslaved persons but also had **intergenerational effects**, shaping the health and well-being of their descendants in Black communities to this day.

Legacy of Oppression in Black Communities

The enduring legacy of oppression in Black communities today can be traced back to the **systemic injustices** perpetuated by slave patrols and their enforcement of brutal and dehumanizing conditions on the enslaved population. The impact of these historical injustices continues to reverberate through generations, shaping the **socio-economic disparities**, **systemic racism**, and **persistent inequalities** faced by Black individuals and communities. The **trauma inflicted** by slave patrols, through violence, surveillance, and control, has left deep scars that persist in the collective memory and experiences of Black Americans.

The legacy of oppression manifests in various facets of modern society, including **disparities in wealth**, education, healthcare, and criminal justice. These disparities reflect the historical marginalization and exploitation of Black communities, perpetuating **cycles of poverty** and disenfranchisement. Additionally, the psychological impact of centuries of oppression has contributed to issues such as higher rates of **mental health challenges** and lower **overall well-being** within Black communities.

Understanding the legacy of oppression is essential for addressing current inequities and working towards a more just and equitable society for all individuals. By acknowledging the historical roots of systemic injustices, we can begin to dismantle **oppressive structures** and work towards true equality and justice.

Continued Influence on Policing Systems

The lasting legacy of **slave patrols** continues to exert a significant influence on **modern policing systems**, shaping policies, practices, and relationships with Black communities. The roots of policing in the United States can be traced back to slave patrols, where the primary objective was to control and oppress Black individuals. This historical context has led to deep-seated issues within law enforcement, including **racial profiling**, **excessive use of force**, and **systemic discrimination** against people of color.

The impact of slave patrols can be seen in contemporary practices such as aggressive policing in **Black neighborhoods, disproportionate rates of arrests** and incarceration among Black individuals, and a **lack of accountability** for police misconduct when it involves Black victims. The inherent bias and racism ingrained in the foundation of policing continue to perpetuate injustices and inequalities in the criminal justice system.

Addressing these systemic issues requires a thorough overhaul of policing practices, including increased accountability measures, community policing initiatives, and **anti-bias training** for law enforcement officers. Only through acknowledging and actively combating the historical influences of slave patrols can meaningful progress be made towards creating a more equitable and just policing system for all communities.

Conclusion

To sum up, the legacy of slave patrols in America is a dark shadow that continues to haunt black communities to this day.

Like a sinister specter, the impact of these patrols can be seen in the continued oppression and **systemic racism** within policing systems.

The **psychological and physical trauma** inflicted on enslaved individuals, as well as their acts of resistance and escapes, serve as a reminder of the **enduring effects** of this brutal chapter in history.

Examination of Notable Legal Cases Involving Slave Patrols

The legal cases involving slave patrols reveal the systematic control over enslaved individuals and the legal complexities surrounding slavery in the U.S. **Dred Scott V. Sandford** denied freedom to enslaved individuals, sparking the tensions leading to the Civil War. **Prigg V. Pennsylvania** highlighted the clash between states' rights and federal authority. **State V. Mann** regulated patroller conduct and showcased legal intricacies in the antebellum South. Nat Turner's Rebellion intensified patrols' aggression. This glimpse into notable cases underscores the depths of legal battles shaping America's history.

Key Takeaways

- Dred Scott v. Sandford denied freedom claims, stating African Americans had no rights.
- Prigg v. Pennsylvania upheld federal supremacy over state laws on slavery enforcement.
- State v. Mann ruled in favor of slave owners, regulating patrollers' conduct.
- Legal cases highlighted complexities in the antebellum South regarding slavery.
- Nat Turner's Rebellion led to increased vigilance and aggression by slave patrols.

Legal Justifications for Patrols

The legal justifications for the establishment and operation of **slave patrols** in colonial America were rooted in maintaining control over enslaved populations and preserving the **economic interests** of slave owners and the broader society. Slave patrols were seen as necessary to **prevent uprisings**, escape attempts, and overall disobedience among the enslaved individuals. The patrols were justified under the premise of protecting the **property rights** of slave owners and ensuring the stability of the institution of slavery.

Additionally, proponents of slave patrols argued that they were essential for safeguarding **public safety** by enforcing curfews, regulating movement, and suppressing any resistance from the enslaved population. The legal framework supporting slave patrols often drew upon existing laws related to property rights and the **regulation of labor**. These justifications provided a legal basis for the systematic surveillance, control, and **violent enforcement methods** employed by slave patrols, perpetuating the oppressive system of slavery in colonial America.

Dred Scott V. Sandford Case

The landmark legal case **Dred Scott v. Sandford** critically examined the status of **enslaved individuals as property** under the law in the United States. Dred Scott, an enslaved man, sued for his freedom on the basis of having lived in free territories.

The Supreme Court's decision in 1857, however, denied Scott's claim, stating that as a person of African descent, he was not a citizen and hence had no right to bring a case to court. **Chief Justice Roger Taney**'s majority opinion went further, asserting that African Americans, whether free or enslaved, could not be considered American citizens and had no rights under the Constitution.

This ruling not only **denied Dred Scott his freedom** but also deepened the divide over slavery in the United States, contributing to the tensions that eventually led to the **Civil War**. The decision in Dred Scott v. Sandford remains one of the most controversial and criticized judgments in **American legal history**.

Prigg V. Pennsylvania Case

In the case of **Prigg v. Pennsylvania**, the legal dispute centered on the enforcement of the **Fugitive Slave Act of 1793** and its implications for states' rights and the institution of slavery in the United States.

The key issue revolved around whether states had the authority to nullify or interfere with federal laws regarding the capture and return of fugitive slaves. **Edward Prigg**, a slave catcher, was charged in Pennsylvania for capturing a fugitive slave and taking her to Maryland, which was a violation of Pennsylvania state law.

The **Supreme Court** ultimately ruled in 1842 that states could not pass laws impeding the execution of the Fugitive Slave Act, establishing **federal supremacy** in matters concerning fugitive slaves.

This decision heightened tensions between states advocating for states' rights and those supporting federal authority, setting a precedent that would influence future legal battles surrounding slavery in the United States.

State V. Mann Case

Examining the legal implications of the **State v. Mann** case sheds light on the complexities surrounding the enforcement of slave patrol laws and the treatment of enslaved individuals in the **antebellum South**.

The case, which took place in North Carolina in 1829, involved **John Mann**, a **slave owner**, who sued **John Ashley**, a patroller, for shooting and severely injuring one of his enslaved people, **Lydia**.

The court's decision in this case was controversial as it ruled in favor of the slave owner, asserting that patrollers did not have unlimited power over enslaved individuals and should not inflict excessive violence upon them. However, this ruling did not fundamentally challenge the institution of slavery itself but rather aimed to regulate the conduct of patrollers.

The State v. Mann case highlighted the fine line between maintaining order through **slave patrols** and preventing extreme abuse of power, showcasing the intricate legal landscape that governed the lives of enslaved individuals in the antebellum South.

Impact of Nat Turners Rebellion

The **uprising** led by **Nat Turner** in 1831 not only sparked widespread fear and paranoia among **slaveholders** in the South but also prompted stringent **legislative actions** aimed at further restricting the already limited freedoms of enslaved individuals.

Nat Turner's rebellion, characterized by its **violent nature** and the high number of casualties, sent shockwaves through the Southern states, where the majority of enslaved individuals resided. The revolt led to retaliatory measures by white slave-owners, who sought to maintain control and prevent future uprisings.

In response to the rebellion, states such as Virginia implemented stricter **slave codes**, imposing harsher restrictions on enslaved people's movement, assembly, and access to education. The fear instilled by Nat Turner's rebellion further fueled the vigilance of **slave patrols**, empowering them to act with increased aggression and brutality in the name of preventing **insurrection**.

The impact of Turner's rebellion underscored the tenuous balance of power in the antebellum South and highlighted the deep-seated tensions between enslaved individuals and their oppressors.

Abolition of Slave Patrols

Following the increasing calls for reform and the shifting societal attitudes towards slavery, the era saw a gradual dismantling of the **institution of slave patrols**. As **abolitionist movements** gained traction and the immorality of slavery became more **widely acknowledged**, various states began to abolish or greatly limit the powers of slave patrols. In the North, where slavery was increasingly viewed as incompatible with the values of the new nation, states like Pennsylvania and Massachusetts took steps to **disband their patrol systems**. Even in the South, where the practice of slavery was **deeply entrenched**, some states began to **reduce the authority** and scope of slave patrols in response to growing dissent.

The abolition of slave patrols did not happen overnight but was rather a **slow and contentious process**. While some states moved more swiftly to disband these groups, others resisted change and maintained their patrols well into the mid-19th century. The eventual abolition of slave patrols represented a **significant milestone** in the fight against slavery and the recognition of the inherent rights and dignity of all individuals.

Conclusion

To sum up, the examination of notable legal cases involving slave patrols reveals the complex history and legal justifications behind their existence. These cases, such as **Dred Scott v. Sandford**, **Prigg v. Pennsylvania**, and **State v. Mann**, demonstrate the deep-rooted institutional support for slave patrols.

The impact of Nat Turner's Rebellion ultimately led to the **abolition of slave patrols**, marking a significant shift in the enforcement of slavery laws.

As the adage goes, "history serves as a reminder of the past, shaping the present and future."

Comparative Analysis across Different Regions and Time Periods

A comparative analysis of **slave patrols** reveals **diverse enforcement tactics** and **societal impacts** spanning regions and eras. Different areas like the U.S. South, the Caribbean, and Latin America employed varied control methods. Enslaved communities faced surveillance, fear, and **disruptions to family ties**. Patrol effectiveness depended on economic reliance on slavery and local support. Adaptations to changing societal norms and **resistance levels** shaped patrol strategies. Understanding these nuances exposes the complexities of power dynamics and the lasting influence on modern structures. Examining these dynamics across time and regions exposes a rich tapestry of historical significance.

Key Takeaways

- Enforcement methods varied across regions, with the U.S. having centralized patrols and Latin America decentralized.
- Southern U.S. imposed harsh regulations, while the Caribbean relied on fear tactics for control.
- Adaptation to changing societal norms influenced patrol objectives over time.
- Effectiveness in controlling enslaved populations depended on economic reliance and resistance levels.
- Legacy of slave patrols persists in modern policing, impacting societal structures and perpetuating systemic racism.

Evolution of Patrol Practices

Throughout history, the development of patrol practices has been marked by notable shifts in tactics, strategies, and the underlying motivations driving the **surveillance** and control of **marginalized populations**. From the early **slave patrols** in the American South to modern-day law enforcement agencies, the methods used to monitor and oppress marginalized groups have transformed over time. Initially focused on preventing slave revolts and maintaining the institution of slavery, patrol practices have adapted to serve different purposes as **societal norms** shifted.

As societies progressed, patrol practices evolved to reflect changing ideologies and **power structures**. The shift from overt slave patrols to more **covert forms** of surveillance illustrates this evolution. Additionally, **advancements in technology** have greatly impacted patrol practices, enabling more efficient monitoring and control of populations. The motivations behind these practices have also evolved, from explicitly oppressive aims to purportedly more benevolent goals like public safety and crime prevention. Understanding the evolution of patrol practices provides insight into the complexities of power dynamics and **social control mechanisms** throughout history.

Regional Variations in Enforcement

Examining enforcement practices across different regions reveals nuanced variations in the application and effectiveness of surveillance and control mechanisms.

In the **Southern United States**, where **slave patrols** were most prevalent, enforcement was characterized by **stringent regulations** and **harsh punishments** to maintain control over enslaved populations. Patrollers in this region often worked in close collaboration with slave owners to prevent insurrections and escape attempts.

Conversely, in the **Caribbean**, where plantations were larger and more isolated, enforcement mechanisms were less formalized, relying more on the fear of **brutal punishments** to deter resistance.

Additionally, in **Latin America**, slave patrols operated with a more **decentralized structure**, allowing for greater autonomy at the local level. This variation in enforcement strategies highlights the complex relationship between geography, demographics, and the institution of slavery, demonstrating how different regions adapted their control mechanisms to suit their unique circumstances.

Understanding these regional variations is essential for a thorough analysis of the historical impact of slave patrols on enslaved communities.

Impact on Enslaved Communities

Enforcement practices not only shaped the **dynamics of surveillance and control** within enslaved populations but also profoundly influenced the social fabric and psychological well-being of individuals subjected to the **oppressive regime of slave patrols**.

The constant threat of being monitored, apprehended, and punished by patrols instilled fear and anxiety among the enslaved communities, leading to a **pervasive atmosphere of terror** and submission. The presence of slave patrols restricted the mobility and autonomy of enslaved individuals, disrupting familial and communal ties.

Additionally, the violent methods employed by patrols to maintain control often resulted in **physical and psychological trauma** for those targeted. This **environment of fear and brutality** created a **sense of helplessness and despair** within the enslaved communities, perpetuating a **cycle of trauma and vulnerability**.

The impact of slave patrols extended beyond mere surveillance; it penetrated the very core of enslaved societies, shaping their behaviors, relationships, and mental well-being in profound ways.

Resistance Strategies and Outcomes

Resistance against the **oppressive system** of **slave patrols** was a persistent and multifaceted endeavor undertaken by enslaved individuals across various regions and time periods. Enslaved people employed a range of strategies to resist the dehumanizing effects of slave patrols. Some engaged in **acts of sabotage**, such as breaking tools or feigning illness, to disrupt the patrols' activities. Others utilized more **covert methods**, like forming **secret societies** or networks to share information and coordinate escape attempts. Additionally, resistance took the form of **cultural preservation**, with enslaved communities maintaining traditions, languages, and spiritual practices as a way to assert their humanity and resist the erasure of their identity.

Despite facing severe consequences for their actions, including **violent reprisals** and even death, many enslaved individuals succeeded in their resistance efforts. By challenging the authority of slave patrols and asserting their **agency** in various ways, these acts of resistance contributed to the eventual dismantling of the institution of slavery and the abolition of slave patrols in different parts of the world.

Role in Maintaining Social Order

The role of **slave patrols** in maintaining **social order** within the institution of slavery was pivotal, shaping **power dynamics** and reinforcing the **hierarchical structure** of society.

These patrols were instrumental in upholding the oppressive system by monitoring and controlling the movements of enslaved individuals. By instilling fear and exerting authority through patrols, slave owners aimed to deter any potential uprisings or **acts of resistance** among the enslaved population.

The presence of patrols not only enforced **labor discipline** but also served as a constant reminder of the subjugation faced by enslaved people.

In addition, slave patrols functioned as a means of surveillance, ensuring that slaves adhered to the established norms and regulations set by the dominant white society. The visibility of these patrols in everyday life further entrenched the **social divisions** between the oppressors and the oppressed, perpetuating a climate of fear and subordination.

Comparison of Patrol Structures

Across different regions and time periods, the structures of **slave patrols** exhibited variations in organization and methods of surveillance and control. In the **antebellum South** of the United States, slave patrols were typically organized by **local militias** or groups of white men who were tasked with monitoring and controlling the movements of enslaved individuals. These patrols often operated on horseback, making regular rounds to check plantations and public spaces for any signs of potential **slave rebellions** or escapes.

In the Caribbean, where **sugar plantations** were prevalent, slave patrols were organized by **plantation owners** and overseers, often using brutal methods to maintain control over the enslaved population. In contrast, in Brazil, slave patrols were more **decentralized**, with individual slave owners responsible for monitoring their own slaves. These variations in organization and methods of surveillance reflect the unique social, economic, and political contexts in which slave patrols operated, highlighting the complex nature of slave societies across different regions and time periods.

Effectiveness in Controlling Slaves

In evaluating the **operational efficacy** of slave patrols across diverse regions and historical eras, the focus shifts towards evaluating their effectiveness in controlling enslaved populations under varying circumstances.

The effectiveness of slave patrols in controlling slaves varied notably depending on factors such as the **economic reliance on slavery**, the **size of the enslaved population**, and the **level of resistance** among the enslaved individuals.

In regions where slavery was a cornerstone of the economy, patrols were often more extensive and brutal, employing violence and intimidation to **maintain control**. However, in areas where enslaved populations were smaller or resistance was higher, patrols struggled to assert authority, leading to frequent escapes and **acts of rebellion**.

The effectiveness of slave patrols also depended on the support they received from local authorities and communities. In some cases, patrols faced opposition or apathy from **white residents**, undermining their ability to control the enslaved population effectively.

Adaptation to Changing Time Periods

Amid **shifting societal norms** and **evolving legal frameworks**, the adaptation of **slave patrols** to changing time periods necessitated strategic modifications in their operational methods and objectives. As the socio-political landscape transformed over time, slave patrols had to adjust their approaches to maintain control over enslaved populations.

During the early establishment of slave patrols, which coincided with the institutionalization of slavery, their **primary focus** was on surveillance, apprehension, and punishment of runaway slaves. However, with the **gradual abolition of slavery** and the emergence of new laws and regulations, the role of slave patrols shifted towards **enforcing labor discipline**, monitoring compliance with new regulations, and preventing uprisings.

Moreover, as the **abolitionist movement** gained momentum and public opinion turned against slavery, slave patrols had to adapt to increasing scrutiny and resistance. This led to a more **covert operational style**, where patrols disguised themselves or operated at night to evade detection. The evolving landscape of the time required slave patrols to become more clandestine and cunning in their methods to maintain control over the enslaved population amidst **changing societal attitudes** and legal frameworks.

Legacy and Lasting Influences

The **enduring legacy** of **slave patrols** extends beyond their historical context, shaping **societal structures** and perceptions long after their formal disbandment. While formally abolished, the practices and ideologies that underpinned slave patrols have left a lasting impact on the social fabric of various regions. The normalization of **surveillance, control, and violence** against **marginalized groups**, which were central to the operations of slave patrols, has seeped into law enforcement agencies and societal attitudes. This legacy manifests in the **disproportionate targeting** and mistreatment of minority communities by modern policing systems.

Furthermore, the racial biases ingrained in slave patrols have persisted through generations, contributing to **systemic racism** and inequality in contemporary societies. The deep-rooted distrust and fear of authority figures among minority populations can be traced back to the oppressive tactics employed by slave patrols. The enduring influence of slave patrols underscores the importance of critically examining historical practices to understand their implications on present-day social structures and to work towards dismantling **oppressive systems**.

Conclusion

To sum up, the comparative analysis of **slave patrols** reveals a complex and multifaceted system of control that varied considerably across different regions and time periods. Despite their differences, these patrols shared common goals of **maintaining order** and enforcing the **institution of slavery**.

Like two sides of the same coin, the evolution and impact of slave patrols can be likened to a double-edged sword, shaping the experiences of enslaved communities and leaving a lasting imprint on the history of oppression.

CHAPTER 7: CULTURAL AND SOCIETAL IMPACT OF SLAVE PATROLS

Slave Patrols Influence on Racial Attitudes and Stereotypes

The historical legacy of **slave patrols** profoundly influenced **racial attitudes** and stereotypes in the United States. These patrols, comprised of armed white men, enforced societal perceptions of race and power dynamics. They perpetuated the belief in the inferiority of Black individuals, instilling fear within enslaved communities and reinforcing **negative stereotypes**. The impact of slave patrols extended to modern policing systems, raising questions about biases and discriminatory practices. This complex history continues to shape **systemic racism** and discrimination, prompting critical reflections on the origins of racial inequalities.

Key Takeaways

- Shaped societal perceptions of race and power dynamics.
- Reinforced belief in inherent inferiority of Black people.
- Instilled fear among enslaved communities.
- Constant surveillance emphasized subservient status.
- Maintained social order placing white people at the top.

Role in Enforcing Racial Hierarchies

Playing a pivotal role in shaping **societal perceptions of race** and reinforcing existing power dynamics, **slave patrols** in the Southern United States wielded a significant influence on the enforcement of **racial hierarchies**. These patrols were not just about capturing escaped slaves but also about **maintaining the social order** that placed white people at the top and Black people at the bottom. By actively surveilling, controlling, and punishing enslaved individuals, slave patrols helped solidify the belief in the **inherent inferiority of Black people**, perpetuating stereotypes that justified their subjugation.

Moreover, the **visible presence of armed patrols** instilled fear among enslaved communities, reminding them of their vulnerable position within the racial hierarchy. The patrols' authority to stop, search, and interrogate any Black person further emphasized their subservient status and lack of autonomy. This **constant surveillance and control** reinforced the racial boundaries and power differentials, ensuring that the hierarchy remained intact and unchallenged. The legacy of these patrols continues to influence racial attitudes and power structures in the present day, highlighting the **enduring impact of their role** in enforcing racial hierarchies.

Impact on Black Community

Having perpetuated the belief in **Black inferiority** and **enforced racial subjugation** through **surveillance and control**, **slave patrols** in the Southern United States profoundly impacted the Black community, shaping their experiences and opportunities within the oppressive racial hierarchy.

The presence of slave patrols instilled fear and anxiety among enslaved individuals, creating a constant state of surveillance and control that restricted their movements and autonomy. This environment of fear not only limited the physical freedom of Black individuals but also had **lasting psychological effects**, perpetuating feelings of powerlessness and inferiority within the community.

Moreover, the actions of slave patrols led to the reinforcement of **negative stereotypes** about Black people, portraying them as inherently criminal or dangerous. These stereotypes, rooted in the **dehumanization and oppression** of enslaved individuals, continue to influence perceptions of the Black community today.

The impact of slave patrols on the Black community extended beyond physical harm, contributing to the **systemic racism** and discrimination that persist in contemporary society. Understanding this historical context is essential for recognizing and addressing the **enduring effects** of slavery on racial attitudes and disparities in the United States.

Relationship to Modern Policing

In examining the historical legacy of **slave patrols**, it becomes evident that their practices and ideologies have significantly influenced the evolution and structure of **modern policing** systems in the United States.

The origins of modern policing in the U.S. can be traced back to the early establishment of slave patrols in the South. The primary function of slave patrols was to maintain control over enslaved populations, prevent revolts, and uphold the **institution of slavery**. These patrols laid the foundation for the development of law enforcement agencies, shaping their role in society.

The **hierarchical structure**, **authoritarian practices**, and focus on **surveillance and control** that characterized slave patrols have persisted in modern policing. The emphasis on maintaining order, exerting authority, and targeting specific **marginalized communities** reflects a continuation of the oppressive tactics employed by slave patrols. This historical connection raises important questions about the inherent biases and discriminatory practices embedded within modern policing systems.

Recognizing this link is vital in understanding the roots of **systemic racism** and injustice that persist in law enforcement today.

Perpetuation of Racial Stereotypes

The perpetuation of **racial stereotypes** within **modern policing** continues to be a significant issue rooted in the **historical legacy** of slave patrols and their impact on **law enforcement practices** in the United States. Despite advances in **civil rights** and **diversity training**, stereotypes deeply ingrained in society persist within some police departments. These stereotypes often portray people of color, especially Black individuals, as inherently dangerous, criminal, or suspicious. Such biased perceptions can lead to **racial profiling**, **excessive use of force**, and **discriminatory practices**.

Studies have shown that these stereotypes not only influence individual officers' behavior but also shape institutional policies and procedures. For example, the over-policing of minority communities and the disproportionate rates of arrest and incarceration among people of color reflect these underlying biases. The media's portrayal of crime and policing further reinforces these stereotypes, perpetuating a cycle of mistrust and tension between law enforcement and marginalized communities.

Addressing the perpetuation of racial stereotypes within policing requires a multifaceted approach that includes ongoing training on implicit bias, community engagement, and accountability measures to challenge and change these harmful narratives.

Dehumanization of Enslaved Individuals

The historical legacy of **slave patrols** in the United States not only perpetuated **racial stereotypes** within modern policing but also played a significant role in the **dehumanization** of enslaved individuals. Enslaved individuals were treated as property rather than as human beings, stripped of their autonomy, dignity, and basic rights. The **institutionalized violence** and control exerted by slave patrols reinforced the notion that enslaved individuals were mere commodities, devoid of agency or **personhood**.

Dehumanization was an essential tactic employed to justify the brutal treatment inflicted upon enslaved individuals. By portraying them as **subhuman** or inherently inferior, slave owners and patrollers sought to rationalize their **exploitation and abuse**. This degrading portrayal not only affected how enslaved individuals were perceived by society at large but also influenced how they viewed themselves, internalizing the dehumanizing narratives imposed upon them.

Understanding the dehumanization of enslaved individuals within the context of slave patrols is vital in comprehending the lasting impact of systemic racism and injustice. It underscores the **deep-rooted biases** and prejudices that continue to shape societal attitudes towards **marginalized communities** today.

Influence on Legal System

Exerting a profound influence on the legal system, **slave patrols** in the United States shaped the development of laws and policies that perpetuated **racial inequality** and oppression. These patrols were instrumental in maintaining the institution of slavery by enforcing laws that controlled the movement and behavior of enslaved individuals. The **legal framework** surrounding slave patrols not only sanctioned the brutal treatment of enslaved people but also reinforced the idea of white superiority and Black inferiority.

The legacy of slave patrols can be seen in the post-Emancipation period through the implementation of **Black Codes** and **Jim Crow laws**, which continued to restrict the rights and freedoms of African Americans. The discriminatory practices ingrained in the legal system by slave patrols persisted even after slavery was abolished, leading to **systemic racism** in law enforcement, the judicial system, and other facets of society.

Resistance and Repercussions

With the **abolition of slavery**, resistance against the **oppressive legacy of slave patrols** emerged, sparking repercussions that reverberated throughout American society. As African Americans fought for their rights and dignity, they faced severe backlash from those who sought to maintain the status quo of racial hierarchy. The resistance took various forms, including **civil rights movements**, protests, and legal challenges to **discriminatory laws**. These actions led to significant changes in legislation and public opinion, challenging the **deeply ingrained racial attitudes** and stereotypes perpetuated by slave patrols.

The repercussions of this resistance were profound. While progress was made in **dismantling overtly racist laws** and practices, the underlying biases and prejudices remained deeply entrenched in American society. The resistance against the oppressive legacy of slave patrols highlighted the need for continued efforts to address **systemic racism and inequality**. It also brought to light the enduring impact of **historical injustices** on contemporary racial dynamics. Moving forward, it is essential to acknowledge the resistance against slave patrols as an important chapter in the ongoing struggle for racial justice and equality.

Racial Bias in Justice System

In examining the justice system, a prevalent issue that demands critical analysis is the pervasive presence of **racial bias**. Racial bias in the justice system manifests in various forms, including **disparities in arrest rates**, **sentencing lengths**, and overall treatment of individuals based on their race. Studies have consistently shown that individuals from **marginalized racial groups**, particularly Black and Hispanic communities, are **disproportionately targeted** and subjected to harsher treatment within the criminal justice system compared to their white counterparts. This **systemic bias** not only undermines the principle of equality before the law but also perpetuates harmful stereotypes and reinforces existing power dynamics that disadvantage minority communities.

The **overrepresentation of people of color** in prisons and the **unequal application of laws** highlight the deep-rooted racial biases that continue to plague the justice system. These biases not only impact the lives of those directly involved but also erode trust in the fairness and impartiality of the legal system as a whole. Addressing and rectifying these ingrained prejudices is essential to ensuring a more just and equitable society for all individuals, regardless of their race or ethnicity.

Addressing Historical Trauma

To effectively address the enduring impact of **historical trauma** on **marginalized communities**, a thorough and nuanced approach must be undertaken that acknowledges the **deep-rooted injustices** of the past. Historical trauma refers to the long-lasting emotional and psychological wounds resulting from significant events that have taken place in the history of a community or population.

In the context of slavery and the **legacy of slave patrols** in the United States, the trauma experienced by Black communities continues to reverberate through generations. Addressing historical trauma requires more than just surface-level acknowledgment; it necessitates a detailed understanding of how past injustices have shaped present-day realities.

Recognizing historical trauma involves creating spaces for individuals to process **intergenerational pain** and fostering healing through **culturally sensitive practices**. Furthermore, it entails implementing policies that redress historical injustices and actively working to dismantle systems that **perpetuate inequality**.

Conclusion

To summarize, the **historical legacy** of slave patrols continues to influence racial attitudes and perpetuate stereotypes in modern society.

One interesting statistic to ponder is that a study by the ACLU found that African Americans are incarcerated at a rate five times higher than white Americans, highlighting the ongoing **racial bias** in the justice system.

It is essential for society to acknowledge and address the **deep-rooted impact** of slave patrols on our present-day understanding of race and policing.

Slave Patrols Perpetuation of Inequality and Social Hierarchies

Slave patrols in America emerged to enforce control over enslaved individuals, perpetuating entrenched inequalities and reinforcing **social hierarchies**. Their existence highlighted power dynamics and the subjugation of marginalized groups, shaping societal structures that endure today. Understanding the impact of these patrols is essential in comprehending **systemic injustices** and historical oppressions. The role they played in maintaining order through fear and coercion underscores the ongoing struggle for equality and justice. Expanding knowledge on this topic reveals deeper insights into the complexities of our societal framework and the importance of challenging **oppressive systems**.

Key Takeaways

- Slave patrols reinforced social hierarchies by enforcing control over enslaved individuals.
- They upheld economic interests of slave owners, perpetuating inequality.
- Maintained power dynamics to subjugate and instill fear in the enslaved population.
- Contributed to the enduring struggle against systemic injustices for equality.
- Perpetuated a culture of fear and compliance to reinforce the racial hierarchy.

Role in Enforcing Inequality

The historical development of **slave patrols** reveals their pivotal role in perpetuating **social hierarchies** and reinforcing **systemic inequalities** within American society. These patrols were instrumental in maintaining the **subjugation of enslaved individuals** by upholding the **power dynamics** of the time. By actively monitoring and controlling the movements of enslaved people, slave patrols guaranteed that any attempts at **resistance or escape** were swiftly quashed, further entrenching the divide between the oppressors and the oppressed.

Enforcing inequality was at the core of the slave patrol's existence, as they sought to uphold the **economic interests** of slave owners and preserve the **racial hierarchy** that justified the dehumanization of Black individuals. The very presence of these patrols served as a constant reminder of the subordinate status assigned to enslaved people, **perpetuating a culture of fear** and compliance that reinforced the existing social order.

Through their actions and authority, slave patrols not only maintained the institution of slavery but also contributed to the deep-rooted inequalities that continue to impact society today. The legacy of these patrols underscores the enduring struggle against systemic injustices and the ongoing quest for equality and justice for all.

Tactics and Methods Used

Utilizing a range of **coercive tactics** and **surveillance methods**, slave patrols operated as a formidable force in enforcing control and instilling fear among the enslaved population, thereby solidifying their subservient status within the societal framework.

These patrols employed strategies such as regular **armed patrols**, where groups of armed men would traverse plantations, roads, and public spaces to monitor and intimidate enslaved individuals. Additionally, they utilized **harsh physical punishments**, such as whipping or branding, to maintain order and deter any thoughts of resistance.

The patrols also relied on **psychological tactics**, instilling a **constant state of fear** and uncertainty among the enslaved community through random inspections, curfews, and restrictions on movement. By employing these methods, slave patrols sought to assert dominance and reinforce the **power dynamics** that upheld the institution of slavery.

Understanding these tactics is essential in comprehending the oppressive nature of slave patrols and the profound impact they had on the lives of enslaved individuals.

Impact on Enslaved Individuals

How did the **relentless presence** and **oppressive tactics** of slave patrols shape the psychological well-being and **sense of agency** among the enslaved individuals they targeted?

The constant fear instilled by the patrols, which had the authority to stop, question, and use violence against any enslaved person, created a **pervasive atmosphere of terror** and powerlessness. Enslaved individuals lived under the constant threat of being separated from their families, subjected to physical punishment, or even killed for perceived acts of defiance. This **environment of surveillance** and violence not only eroded their mental well-being but also stripped away their autonomy and sense of self-worth.

Moreover, the **psychological impact** of being constantly surveilled and dehumanized by slave patrols cannot be overstated. Enslaved individuals **internalized feelings of inferiority** and helplessness, as they were reminded daily of their status as property rather than as human beings deserving of dignity and respect.

This deep psychological trauma inflicted by slave patrols continues to reverberate through generations, highlighting the **enduring legacy** of systemic oppression and the dehumanization of enslaved individuals.

Relationship to Social Hierarchies

The insidious presence of **slave patrols** entrenched and reinforced **existing social hierarchies** by **perpetuating power differentials** and **maintaining control** over **marginalized communities**.

These patrols, sanctioned by laws and societal norms, not only **upheld the institution of slavery** but also perpetuated a system where certain groups held dominance over others. Enslaved individuals were at the mercy of these patrols, which symbolized the **authority of the slave-owning class** and enforced a **rigid social order** that oppressed those deemed inferior.

Moreover, the relationship between slave patrols and social hierarchies extended beyond the physical control of enslaved individuals. It created a psychological environment of fear and submission, where the threat of violence and punishment loomed large, further solidifying the power dynamics within society.

This **normalization of oppression** and subjugation had far-reaching consequences, shaping societal attitudes and behaviors for generations to come.

Understanding this historical context sheds light on the deep-rooted inequalities that persist in our present-day social structures. By recognizing the role of slave patrols in perpetuating social hierarchies, we can work towards dismantling systems of oppression and fostering a more equitable society for all.

Resistance and Rebellions

Resistance against the oppressive system enforced by **slave patrols** was a courageous act of defiance that challenged the status quo and sparked movements for liberation among the marginalized communities. Enslaved individuals, despite facing severe consequences, displayed remarkable bravery in their efforts to resist the **dehumanizing practices** of slave patrols. These **acts of resistance** took various forms, including sabotage, escape attempts, and uprisings. One of the most notable rebellions was the **Stono Rebellion** of 1739 in South Carolina, where a group of enslaved Africans seized weapons, killed several whites, and attempted to flee to Spanish Florida.

Resistance was not limited to physical acts of rebellion; it also encompassed subtle forms of defiance, such as maintaining **cultural practices**, preserving languages, and nurturing community ties. Through these acts of resistance, enslaved individuals asserted their humanity and agency in the face of **systematic oppression**. The legacy of these acts of resistance continues to inspire movements for **social justice** and equality today.

Legacy in Modern Society

Within contemporary society, the **enduring legacy** of enslaved individuals' **acts of resistance** against slave patrols reverberates through **ongoing struggles** for **social justice** and equality. The resistance displayed by these individuals against oppressive systems continues to inspire movements that challenge discrimination and promote inclusivity. The determination and courage shown by those who fought against the **dehumanizing practices** of slave patrols serve as a poignant reminder of the resilience of the human spirit in the face of adversity.

Moreover, the legacy of these acts of resistance highlights the importance of recognizing and addressing historical injustices in the quest for a more equitable society. By acknowledging the past struggles of marginalized communities, we can better understand the **systemic inequalities** that persist today and work towards dismantling them. The lessons learned from the resistance against slave patrols underscore the significance of solidarity and **collective action** in creating lasting social change. As we navigate the complexities of modern society, honoring the legacy of those who resisted oppression can guide us in our ongoing **pursuit of justice** and equality.

Intersectionality of Oppression

As we reflect on the enduring impact of **historical resistance against oppressive systems**, it becomes evident that **exploring the Intersectionality of oppression** is fundamental for understanding the complexities of systemic inequalities within contemporary societies. Intersectionality recognizes that individuals can experience **multiple forms of oppression simultaneously** based on their various social identities such as race, gender, class, sexuality, and more.

In the context of slave patrols and their lasting effects, it is essential to acknowledge how different marginalized groups intersect in their experiences of oppression.

Understanding intersectionality helps us grasp the **interconnected nature of discrimination** and how it operates across different **societal structures**. For example, the legacy of slave patrols not only **perpetuated racial injustice** but also reinforced gender norms and economic disparities. By delving into the intersectionality of oppression, we can better comprehend how these systems intertwine to create and **perpetuate inequalities**.

Psychological Effects on Enslaved

The **psychological effects** experienced by enslaved individuals under the **oppressive system of slavery** were profound and far-reaching, permeating every aspect of their well-being and sense of self. Enslaved individuals were subjected to constant **dehumanization, violence, and degradation**, which had severe consequences on their mental health. The **trauma of being owned**, controlled, and treated as property led to feelings of helplessness, worthlessness, and a distorted sense of identity.

Additionally, the constant threat of punishment, separation from family members, and the denial of basic human rights created a **pervasive atmosphere of fear** and anxiety among the enslaved population.

Many enslaved individuals suffered from depression, anxiety, post-traumatic stress disorder, and other **mental health conditions** as a result of their **traumatic experiences**. The **psychological scars of slavery** were often passed down through generations, impacting the mental well-being of descendants as well. Understanding the deep psychological wounds inflicted by slavery is vital in comprehending the lasting effects of this oppressive system on individuals and communities.

Strategies for Addressing Historical Injustice

Addressing the legacy of **historical injustice** requires a vital approach that acknowledges the **enduring impact** of past atrocities on present-day societal structures and individuals. To begin, education plays a pivotal role in understanding and rectifying historical injustices. Incorporating thorough and accurate accounts of past atrocities in **educational curricula** fosters empathy, critical thinking, and a commitment to social justice among future generations.

Additionally, **reparative measures**, such as offering formal apologies, restitution, and **memorialization efforts**, are essential steps in acknowledging past wrongs and promoting healing within affected communities.

Furthermore, establishing **truth and reconciliation commissions** can provide a platform for victims to share their experiences, **hold perpetrators accountable**, and work towards reconciliation. Engaging in constructive dialogue, promoting inclusivity, and actively challenging **discriminatory practices** are necessary in dismantling the entrenched systems perpetuated by historical injustices. By collectively confronting uncomfortable truths and committing to meaningful action, societies can work towards a more just and equitable future for all.

Conclusion

To sum up, the **perpetuation of inequality** and **social hierarchies** through slave patrols has had lasting effects on marginalized communities.

How can we address the historical injustices and **systemic oppression** that continue to impact society today?

By examining the origins, tactics, and impact of slave patrols, we can better understand the intersectionality of oppression and work towards creating a more equitable and just society for all.

Cultural Memory and Representation of Slave Patrols in Art and Literature

The portrayal of slave patrols in art and literature illuminates the harsh realities of **systemic oppression** and violence faced by enslaved individuals in the American South. Paintings depict armed patrols enforcing control with brutality, while literature evokes empathy through **vivid descriptions** of **dehumanization**. Symbols like chains and watchtowers in artistic representations signify bondage, surveillance, and resistance. While early narratives often glorified these patrols, contemporary explorations offer nuanced and critical perspectives. The legacy of slave patrol imagery continues to influence modern **social justice movements**, drawing parallels between past injustices and current societal power dynamics. Explore further to understand the profound impact on **collective memory**.

Key Takeaways

- Art and literature depict slave patrols to evoke empathy and critical reflection on brutality.
- Symbols like chains and watchtowers in art symbolize oppression and control.
- Contemporary artists offer more nuanced and diverse perspectives on slave patrol narratives.
- Legacy of slave patrol imagery influences modern social justice movements.
- Collective memory surrounding slave patrols prompts critical examination of systemic oppression and power dynamics.

Depiction of Slave Patrols in Paintings

Depicted in various artworks throughout history, the representation of **slave patrols** in **paintings** serves as a poignant reflection of the **oppressive nature** and historical significance of these enforcement groups in the American South. Artists have depicted slave patrols in various ways, capturing the brutality and **power dynamics** inherent in their operations. Paintings often show **armed patrols** mounted on horseback, instilling fear and control over enslaved individuals. The use of dark and **somber tones** in these artworks conveys the somber reality of the violence and intimidation that characterized the actions of slave patrols.

One notable example is the painting 'Slave Patrol' by Hale Woodruff, which **starkly portrays** a group of armed white men on horseback overseeing a group of enslaved individuals working in the fields. The painting's composition and use of contrast highlight the stark power imbalances and the looming threat that slave patrols posed to the enslaved population. Through such **visual representations**, artists bring to light the harsh realities faced by those subjected to the control of these patrols, ensuring that this dark chapter of history is not forgotten.

Impact of Literature on Cultural Memory

Literature plays a crucial role in shaping the **cultural memory** surrounding **historical events** and **societal structures**. Through various forms such as novels, poems, and essays, literature has the power to illuminate aspects of history that might be overlooked or forgotten. In the context of **slave patrols**, literature has been instrumental in both preserving and challenging the narratives surrounding this dark chapter in history. Authors have used their works to vividly depict the brutality and **dehumanization** inflicted by slave patrols, ensuring that these stories are not erased from **collective memory**.

Moreover, literature has the ability to evoke empathy and provoke critical reflection on the **lasting**

impacts of slave patrols on individuals and society as a whole. By delving into the personal experiences of those affected by slave patrols, literature humanizes the victims and underscores the pervasive legacy of racism and oppression. Through its nuanced storytelling and **emotional depth**, literature contributes significantly to shaping how we remember and understand the role of slave patrols in shaping American history.

Symbolism in Artistic Representations

Artistic representations of historical events like **slave patrols** often employ symbolism to convey deeper meanings and provoke contemplation on the enduring impact of such practices. Through the use of **symbols**, artists can encapsulate complex themes and emotions, inviting viewers to engage with the subject matter on a more profound level. In the context of slave patrols, artists may utilize symbols such as **chains** to represent the bondage and oppression experienced by enslaved individuals, or a watchtower to symbolize **surveillance and control**.

Moreover, artists may incorporate symbols of **resistance and resilience**, such as broken chains or a setting sun suggestive of liberation and hope. These symbols serve to not only depict the harsh realities of slave patrols but also to highlight the strength and courage of those who resisted such **systems of control**.

Evolution of Artistic Narratives

The evolution of **storytelling through visual mediums** has played a significant role in shaping **societal perceptions** and understanding of historical events such as slave patrols. Over time, artistic narratives depicting slave patrols have evolved in complexity and depth, reflecting changing societal attitudes and **historical reinterpretations**.

Early artistic representations often depicted slave patrols in a **glorified or heroic light**, reinforcing power dynamics and justifying oppressive practices. As society progressed, artists began to challenge these **romanticized portrayals**, delving into the harsh realities faced by enslaved individuals and the brutality of the institution of slavery.

Artistic narratives have shifted towards more nuanced and critical explorations of slave patrols, highlighting the **violence, fear, and dehumanization** that characterized these groups. Contemporary artists have started to incorporate **diverse perspectives**, including voices from marginalized communities, offering a more inclusive and accurate portrayal of the impacts of slave patrols.

Critique of Romanticized Portrayals

Portrayals of **slave patrols** in early artistic renditions often romanticized the **oppressive nature** of their existence, obscuring the true brutality and violence inflicted upon enslaved individuals. These depictions tended to portray slave patrollers as noble figures carrying out a necessary duty rather than acknowledging the **dehumanizing and terrorizing** aspects of their actions. By romanticizing these patrols, artists and writers perpetuated a **distorted view of history** that downplayed the suffering of enslaved people. This **romanticized portrayal** not only **sanitized the reality** of slave patrols but also perpetuated **harmful stereotypes** and misconceptions about the institution of slavery.

Critiquing these romanticized portrayals is essential to confront the uncomfortable truths of the past and challenge the **glorification of oppressive systems**. By unpacking the romanticized imagery surrounding slave patrols, we can begin to dismantle the idealized narratives that have long dominated cultural representations. It is essential to engage critically with historical artworks and literature to uncover the harsh realities that have been glossed over in favor of a more palatable narrative.

Resonance of Slave Patrol Imagery

The enduring resonance of imagery associated with **slave patrols** reflects a complex interplay between historical representation and contemporary societal perceptions of authority and control. The visual depictions of slave patrols, often portraying **white men on horseback** overseeing and intimidating black individuals **evoke a sense of fear**, oppression, and the **abuse of power**. These images serve as a stark reminder of a **dark chapter in history** when marginalized communities were subjected to systematic violence and surveillance in the name of maintaining order and upholding oppressive systems.

The continued presence of slave patrol imagery in art and literature underscores the **lasting impact** of these historical practices on **modern consciousness**. By confronting these representations, society is forced to reckon with the **enduring legacy of racial injustice** and the ways in which systems of control have evolved over time. These images challenge viewers to question the nature of authority, interrogate power dynamics, and confront the uncomfortable truths of our collective past. Ultimately, the resonance of slave patrol imagery serves as a potent symbol of the ongoing struggle for justice, equality, and liberation in contemporary society.

Influence on Modern Social Justice Movements

The legacy of **slave patrol imagery** exerts a palpable influence on the ethos and strategies of modern social justice movements. The historical context of slave patrols, rooted in the **violent enforcement of racial hierarchies** and the control of marginalized communities, resonates with contemporary struggles for equality and justice. Activists draw parallels between past injustices and current systemic issues, utilizing the memory of slave patrols to highlight the persistent nature of oppression and discrimination.

The **tactics employed by slave patrols**, such as surveillance, intimidation, and violence, find echoes in **present-day policing practices** and **societal power dynamics**. This awareness informs the approaches taken by **social justice advocates**, influencing their calls for police reform, racial equity, and the dismantling of oppressive structures. By acknowledging the **historical roots of injustice** embodied by slave patrols, modern movements aim to challenge existing power structures and advocate for transformative change.

Reflections on Collective Memory

Examination of the **cultural memory** surrounding slave patrols reveals profound insights into the collective consciousness regarding **historical injustices** and their enduring impact on societal structures. **Collective memory** refers to the shared pool of information held by a group of people that shapes their identity, values, and understanding of the past. In the case of slave patrols, the collective memory underscores the **systemic oppression** and violence that were integral to the maintenance of slavery. This memory is not just a recollection of events but a reflection of how societies grapple with their dark histories and the implications for **contemporary social relations**.

The reflection on collective memory sheds light on how **narratives of the past** are constructed, preserved, and transmitted through generations. It also prompts critical examination of **power dynamics**, privilege, and the ways in which historical injustices continue to manifest in present-day structures. By engaging with collective memory, individuals and societies can confront uncomfortable truths, challenge **dominant narratives**, and work towards a more inclusive and just future.

Conclusion

In the tapestry of cultural memory, the representation of **slave patrols** in art and literature serves as a poignant allegory for the **enduring legacy** of systemic oppression and resistance.

Through critical examination of artistic narratives, we uncover the layers of symbolism and critique embedded in these depictions.

As modern **social justice movements** continue to draw inspiration from this historical imagery, it prompts us to reflect on our collective memory and the ongoing struggle for justice and equality.

CHAPTER 8: LEGACY AND RECKONING

Repercussions of Slave Patrols on Contemporary Society

The repercussions of **slave patrols** on contemporary society are evident in persistent **racial bias**, disparities in law enforcement, and **systemic injustices** facing communities of color today. These historical practices have shaped modern policing, leading to **disproportionate targeting**, arrests, and systemic racism within the **criminal justice system**. Understanding this legacy is essential to address the deep-rooted issues affecting marginalized groups. Calls for reform, training, accountability, and community engagement are vital steps towards creating an equitable society. By examining the historical context of slave patrols, we gain insight into the challenges faced by law enforcement and communities today.

Key Takeaways

- Persistent racial bias in law enforcement stems from historical slave patrols.
- Communities of color face higher levels of surveillance and aggressive policing.
- Over-policing leads to disproportionate rates of arrests in communities of color.
- Systemic injustices contribute to marginalization and disenfranchisement.
- Addressing deep-rooted issues requires thorough reforms within law enforcement.

Historical Roots of Modern Policing

Historically, the evolution of modern policing can be traced back to the establishment of **slave patrols** in the **Southern United States** during the 18th and 19th centuries. These patrols were created to maintain control over enslaved populations, **prevent revolts**, and protect the **economic interests** of slave owners. The concept of organized groups monitoring and controlling specific populations laid the groundwork for what would eventually become **formalized law enforcement agencies**.

Slave patrols were the precursor to modern police forces in the United States, **shaping the structure**, functions, and mentality of law enforcement. The practices and attitudes developed during this period continue to influence policing methods today. Understanding this historical context is crucial in comprehending the complexities and challenges faced by law enforcement in contemporary society.

The legacy of slave patrols can be seen in issues such as **racial bias**, unequal treatment, and **systemic discrimination** within the criminal justice system. By examining the historical roots of modern policing, we can gain insight into the origins of these problems and work towards developing more equitable and just law enforcement practices.

Racial Bias in Law Enforcement

The enduring impact of the historical evolution from slave patrols to modern policing is evident in the persistent issue of **racial bias** within **contemporary law enforcement practices**. Despite advancements in civil rights and diversity initiatives, racial bias continues to permeate various aspects of law enforcement, leading to **disparities in the treatment** of individuals based on their race or ethnicity.

Research has shown that individuals from **racial minority groups**, particularly Black and Hispanic communities, are disproportionately targeted for police stops, arrests, the use of force, and harsher sentencing compared to their white counterparts. This **systemic bias** not only **erodes trust** between law enforcement agencies and the communities they serve but also perpetuates feelings of injustice and inequality.

Additionally, the legacy of **historical prejudices** and stereotypes associated with certain racial groups further exacerbates these biases, creating a challenging environment for promoting **fair and equitable policing practices**. Addressing racial bias in law enforcement requires a multifaceted approach that involves training, accountability measures, **community engagement**, and policy reforms to make sure that all individuals are treated with dignity and respect under the law.

Impact on Communities of Color

Within contemporary society, the repercussions of **slave patrols** are keenly felt by communities of color, shaping their interactions with law enforcement and perpetuating **systemic inequalities**. The historical legacy of slave patrols, which were established to control and oppress enslaved populations, has left a lasting impact on how law enforcement engages with communities of color today. The inherent **racial biases** embedded in the origins of these patrols have translated into discriminatory practices and unequal treatment towards people of color.

Communities of color often experience higher levels of surveillance, profiling, and **aggressive policing** compared to their white counterparts. This increased scrutiny not only erodes trust between law enforcement and these communities but also perpetuates a cycle of fear and mistrust. The **over-policing** of neighborhoods mainly inhabited by people of color has led to **disproportionate rates** of arrests, convictions, and **harsher sentencing** for minor offenses within these communities.

These systemic injustices contribute to the marginalization and disenfranchisement of communities of color, reinforcing the need for thorough reforms within law enforcement to address these **deep-rooted issues**.

Criminal Justice System Disparities

The disparities within the criminal justice system today reflect the enduring impact of historical slave patrols on the treatment of **communities of color** by law enforcement. Studies show that communities of color are disproportionately targeted, arrested, convicted, and sentenced compared to their white counterparts. This **systemic bias** is deeply rooted in the **historical context of slave patrols** that were tasked with controlling and oppressing Black individuals. The **over-policing of these communities** has led to a cycle of incarceration, poverty, and lack of opportunities for people of color.

Furthermore, research indicates that implicit biases within the criminal justice system contribute to these disparities. Judges, prosecutors, and law enforcement officers may hold prejudiced views that influence their **decision-making processes**, leading to harsher treatment of individuals from **marginalized communities**. This perpetuates a **cycle of injustice** that is difficult to break without

systemic reform and addressing the deep-seated biases that exist within the criminal justice system. Recognizing and actively working to dismantle these disparities is imperative in creating a more equitable and just society for all.

Perpetuation of Systemic Racism

Evident across various societal structures, **systemic racism** persists in insidious ways, permeating institutions and perpetuating inequities for **marginalized communities**. This pervasive issue is deeply rooted in **historical injustices**, such as the practices of slave patrols that targeted Black individuals. While overt forms of racism have diminished over time, **covert manifestations** continue to disadvantage people of color in areas like education, employment, healthcare, and housing.

In the contemporary context, systemic racism is often perpetuated through **implicit biases**, **discriminatory policies**, and **unequal access to resources**. For example, studies show that Black individuals are disproportionately affected by poverty, incarceration rates, police brutality, and limited opportunities for advancement. These disparities highlight the enduring impact of systemic racism on society at large. Additionally, the **lack of representation** and diversity in leadership positions further perpetuates this cycle of inequality.

Addressing systemic racism requires a holistic approach that involves acknowledging historical injustices, dismantling discriminatory practices, and actively promoting equity and inclusivity in all facets of life.

Calls for Police Reform

Systemic racism's enduring influence on societal structures has propelled a growing chorus of demands for thorough reforms within law enforcement agencies, particularly in response to the pressing issue of **Calls for Police Reform**. The longstanding history of policing in the United States, rooted in slave patrols and segregation-era practices, has contributed to the deep-seated issues of **racial bias** and **excessive use of force** within many police departments. Recent high-profile cases of police violence against Black individuals, such as the deaths of George Floyd, Breonna Taylor, and others, have reignited calls for transformative changes in how law enforcement operates.

Calls for Police Reform encompass a range of proposals, including increased accountability measures, **community policing initiatives**, **demilitarization efforts**, **and implicit bias training**, and reallocating funds from law enforcement to social services. Advocates argue that these reforms are essential to address the systemic injustices that disproportionately impact marginalized communities and perpetuate racial disparities in the **criminal justice system**. As pressure mounts from **grassroots movements** and **civil rights organizations**, the need for meaningful and sustainable change within policing practices becomes increasingly evident.

Healing and Moving Forward

Amidst the ongoing discussions on **police reform** and addressing **systemic issues** within law enforcement, the path towards healing and moving forward requires a multifaceted approach that acknowledges **historical legacies** and prioritizes **community-centered solutions**. To foster healing, it is essential to recognize the deep-rooted impact of **historical practices** like slave patrols on contemporary policing. Acknowledging this history is the first step towards building trust and understanding between law enforcement agencies and the communities they serve.

Moving forward necessitates proactive measures to address the systemic issues that perpetuate harm and inequality. Investing in **community policing strategies** that emphasize collaboration, transparency, and accountability can help bridge the gap between law enforcement and marginalized communities. Additionally, promoting diversity and **cultural competency** within police departments can lead to more empathetic and inclusive practices.

Healing and moving forward require a commitment to dismantling **oppressive structures** and fostering environments where all members of society feel safe and valued. By prioritizing community voices, historical awareness, and **equitable policies**, we can begin to rebuild trust and create a more just and harmonious future.

Conclusion

Essential for society to confront and dismantle these harmful legacies in order to truly achieve justice and equality. When examining the impact of **slave patrols** on today's **policing practices**, it is evident that the repercussions on contemporary society are rooted in the historical roots of modern policing, **racial bias** in law enforcement, impact on communities of color, criminal justice system disparities, and perpetuation of **systemic racism**.

Calls for police reform have been made to address these issues and move towards healing and progress. The bottom line is that the apple doesn't fall far from the tree in this regard.

Calls for Acknowledgment, Reparation, and Reconciliation Due to Slave Patrols

Calls for acknowledgment, reparations, and reconciliation due to slave patrols highlight the enduring impact on Black communities and the urgent need to address **systemic injustices**. The historical context reveals the origins of oppression, shaping present-day disparities. Acknowledging the harm caused is crucial in understanding and rectifying **deep-seated inequalities**. Demands for a **public apology** and reparations aim to heal **generational trauma** and promote equity. Through community engagement, policy changes, and a commitment to **restorative justice**, progress towards reconciliation can be made. Exploring these facets exposes the intricate legacy of slave patrols and the path towards a more just society.

Key Takeaways

- Acknowledgment of slave patrols' harm is crucial for understanding systemic injustices.
- Reparations for descendants aim to address generational trauma and economic disparities.
- Reconciliation involves rebuilding trust and making amends for past wrongs.
- Calls for public apology signal a commitment to addressing historical injustices.
- Restorative justice practices focus on healing, accountability, and reconciliation.

Impact on Black Communities Today

The enduring repercussions of **historical slave patrols** persistently shape the **socio-economic landscape** of contemporary Black communities in the United States. The legacy of slave patrols, which were established to control and oppress Black individuals, continues to manifest in various ways today. One significant impact is the **deep-rooted mistrust** between Black communities and law enforcement, stemming from the origins of patrols as precursors to modern policing. This mistrust often leads to strained relationships, feelings of marginalization, and challenges in ensuring **fair treatment under the law**.

Moreover, the historical disenfranchisement and economic exploitation enforced by slave patrols have contributed to **lasting disparities in wealth**, education, and opportunities for Black Americans. These disparities are evident in higher rates of poverty, lower levels of **access to quality education**, and limited **economic mobility within Black communities**. Addressing these disparities requires a thorough understanding of their **historical roots** and a commitment to implementing policies that promote equity and justice for Black individuals and communities.

Acknowledging the Harm Caused

Acknowledging the **historical atrocities** perpetuated by **slave patrols** is vital in understanding the **systemic injustices** that continue to impact Black communities today. Slave patrols were instrumental in maintaining the institution of slavery by controlling and brutalizing enslaved individuals. These patrols enforced **harsh punishments**, instilled fear, and perpetuated a **dehumanizing environment** that has had lasting effects on Black communities. By recognizing the harm caused by slave patrols, we can begin to unravel the **deep-seated roots** of systemic racism and oppression that persist in society.

The acknowledgment of the harm caused by slave patrols also allows for a more thorough understanding of the current disparities faced by Black communities. The legacy of slavery and its enforcement through patrols has contributed to **ongoing issues** such as police brutality, racial profiling, and unequal access to resources. This recognition is an essential step towards addressing the **deep-seated inequalities** that continue to marginalize Black individuals and communities. It is only through acknowledging the past injustices that we can work towards a more equitable and just future for all.

Demands for Public Apology

Demanding a **public apology** for the historical atrocities committed by slave patrols is an important step towards acknowledging the **systemic injustices** that have plagued Black communities for centuries. These demands are rooted in the recognition that the brutal practices of slave patrols were not isolated incidents but part of a **larger system of oppression** that dehumanized and exploited Black individuals. A public apology serves as a significant acknowledgment of the pain and suffering inflicted upon generations of Black people, validating their experiences and affirming their humanity.

Public apologies have the power to **foster healing and reconciliation** by publicly acknowledging past wrongs and expressing remorse. They can also signal a commitment to addressing **historical injustices** and working towards a more **equitable future**. By issuing a public apology for the actions of slave patrols, society can begin to **confront its dark history** and demonstrate a willingness to learn from the mistakes of the past. It is an essential step towards **building trust, understanding**, and ultimately, a more just and inclusive society.

Reparations for Descendants

Rooted in the historical legacy of **systemic oppression** perpetuated by slave patrols, the discussion now turns towards exploring avenues for **reparations** to be extended to descendants affected by these injustices. The impact of slave patrols on African American communities has been profound and enduring, with repercussions that continue to be felt today. It is imperative to acknowledge the **generational trauma** and **economic disparities** that have resulted from centuries of enslavement, segregation, and discriminatory practices.

Reparations for descendants of individuals who suffered under the tyranny of slave patrols can take various forms, including but not limited to **financial compensation**, **educational opportunities**, **healthcare provisions**, and community investments. The goal of reparations is not simply to provide a one-time payment, but to address the **systemic inequalities** that persist in society. By recognizing the historical injustices inflicted upon African Americans and offering tangible reparatory measures, we can take a significant step towards rectifying the wrongs of the past and fostering a more equitable future for all.

Healing and Restorative Justice

In the pursuit of addressing the enduring impact of **historical injustices** inflicted by slave patrols, a critical aspect that warrants examination is the implementation of **healing and restorative justice** measures. Healing and restorative justice focus on repairing harm caused by **systemic oppression** and **promoting healing** for individuals and communities affected by such injustices. **Restorative justice emphasizes accountability**, **reconciliation**, and healing, aiming to address the **root causes of harm** and promote understanding between all parties involved.

By acknowledging the **historical trauma** inflicted by slave patrols and implementing restorative practices, society can begin to heal the deep wounds caused by centuries of oppression and discrimination.

Restorative justice measures may include community dialogue sessions, truth and reconciliation commissions, and reparative programs aimed at addressing the **ongoing impacts** of historical injustices. These initiatives provide spaces for individuals to share their experiences, seek redress, and work towards healing and reconciliation. Through a commitment to healing and restorative justice, communities can move towards a more just and equitable future, fostering understanding and unity in the face of past injustices.

Education on Slave Patrols

An essential component of addressing the **legacy of slave patrols** is the thorough education on their **historical significance** and impact. Slave patrols were organized groups tasked with enforcing discipline upon enslaved populations in the antebellum South. By educating individuals on the origins and functions of these patrols, society can begin to comprehend the paramount **systemic oppression** they represent.

Understanding the historical context of slave patrols is vital in recognizing their role in **perpetuating racial injustices** and inequalities that persist today. Through education, individuals can grasp how slave patrols were instrumental in maintaining the brutal institution of slavery and how their tactics laid the groundwork for **modern policing practices**.

Moreover, educating the public on the history of slave patrols can foster empathy, encourage critical thinking, and promote discussions on race relations and **social justice**. By shedding light on this **dark chapter of American history**, society can take a step towards acknowledging the **enduring consequences** of these oppressive systems and work towards reconciliation and healing.

Community Engagement Initiatives

Efforts to engage the community in discussions and initiatives related to the history and impact of slave patrols can greatly contribute to raising awareness and fostering meaningful dialogue on systemic oppression and racial inequities. **Community engagement** initiatives play an essential role in acknowledging the legacy of slave patrols and their enduring effects on society.

By organizing **workshops, seminars, and public forums**, community members can come together to learn about this dark chapter in history, reflect on its implications, and discuss strategies for promoting justice and equality.

Engagement initiatives can involve collaboration with **local historians, activists, and educators** to provide accurate information and facilitate constructive conversations. These efforts can help **dispel myths**, **challenge misconceptions**, and encourage individuals to **confront uncomfortable truths** about the past.

Additionally, community engagement can empower people to take action towards addressing **present-day injustices** stemming from the legacy of slave patrols. Through dialogue, education, and collective action, communities can work towards healing, reconciliation, and creating a more inclusive and equitable society for all.

Policy Changes and Advocacy

Strategically implementing **policy changes** and advocating for **legislative reforms** can greatly impact dismantling the **systemic structures** rooted in the historical practices of slave patrols. By targeting specific laws and regulations that perpetuate **discriminatory practices** and inequalities, policymakers can address the lingering effects of slave patrols on contemporary society. **Advocacy**

efforts play an important role in raising awareness, mobilizing support, and pressuring decision-makers to prioritize meaningful reforms.

Policy changes can include revising policing strategies to eliminate tactics derived from slave patrol traditions, investing in community-led safety initiatives, and implementing **anti-bias training** for law enforcement personnel. Additionally, advocating for legislative reforms that address **systemic racism**, promote equity, and support **marginalized communities** is essential for creating a more just and inclusive society.

Through strategic collaboration between policymakers, advocacy groups, scholars, and affected communities, meaningful progress can be made in dismantling the legacy of slave patrols. It is essential to continuously evaluate and adjust these policies and advocacy efforts to make sure they effectively address the deep-rooted issues perpetuated by **historical injustices**.

Moving Towards Reconciliation

To address the lasting impacts of **slave patrols** and advance **societal healing**, a pivotal approach towards **reconciliation** is imperative. Reconciliation, in the context of the **historical injustices** perpetuated by slave patrols, involves acknowledging the wrongs committed, taking steps to **make amends**, and working towards **rebuilding trust** and understanding among affected communities. One vital aspect of moving towards reconciliation is the recognition of the systemic nature of oppression and its **enduring effects** on individuals and society as a whole.

Reconciliation efforts should involve meaningful engagement with communities affected by slave patrols, listening to their experiences, and centering their voices in the process. This may include establishing truth and reconciliation commissions, creating educational programs that accurately depict the history of slave patrols, and providing support for initiatives that promote healing and empowerment within these communities.

Conclusion

In summary, the **historical legacy** of slave patrols continues to impact Black communities today, necessitating acknowledgment, reparation, and reconciliation.

Despite potential objections, it is vital to recognize the lasting harm caused by these institutions and take **concrete steps** towards addressing their legacy.

By advocating for public apologies, reparations, education, community engagement, **policy changes**, and reconciliation efforts, we can work towards healing the wounds of the past and building a more **just society** for all.

Steps toward Addressing Systemic Racism Rooted in Slave Patrols

Addressing **systemic racism** tied to slave patrols requires a **multi-faceted approach** encompassing education, policy, and community involvement. From historical awareness to modern impact recognition, **fostering empathy** and challenging bias is vital. **Transformative actions** include reshaping laws, anti-racism training for law enforcement, and advocating for real change. Building solidarity, understanding diverse voices, and actively supporting **marginalized communities** are essential steps. Together, we can confront the enduring effects of systemic racism and work towards a more just society. Your journey to combat systemic racism and its roots in slave patrols begins with understanding, empathy, and proactive measures.

Key Takeaways

- Implement anti-racism training for law enforcement to address biases and discriminatory practices.
- Establish oversight committees to monitor and address racial bias within law enforcement agencies.
- Advocate for legislative adjustments to reshape laws perpetuating systemic racism.
- Amplify marginalized voices and hold institutions accountable for perpetuating racial inequalities.
- Foster empathy, understanding, and critical thinking through education to challenge systemic racism.

Recognizing Modern-Day Impacts

Exploring the enduring repercussions of historical **slave patrols** sheds light on the pervasive influence of **systemic racism** in contemporary society. The legacy of slave patrols continues to shape many aspects of modern life, impacting **marginalized communities** disproportionately. One modern-day impact is evident in the **criminal justice system**, where **racial profiling** and **biased policing practices** perpetuate inequality. Communities of color often experience higher rates of surveillance, arrests, and harsher sentencing compared to their white counterparts. This unequal treatment not only denies individuals their rights but also perpetuates cycles of poverty and disenfranchisement.

Moreover, the **educational system** reflects the modern-day effects of systemic racism rooted in slave patrols. Racial disparities in school discipline, academic achievement, and access to quality education persist, contributing to the perpetuation of inequity across generations. Recognizing these modern-day impacts is essential in dismantling systemic racism and fostering a more just and inclusive society. By acknowledging the **lasting effects** of historical injustices, we can work towards creating meaningful change and promoting equality for all members of society.

Education and Awareness Initiatives

Education and **awareness initiatives** play a pivotal role in challenging and dismantling **systemic racism** rooted in **historical injustices** like **slave patrols**. By educating individuals about the origins and pervasive impact of systemic racism, these initiatives aim to foster empathy, understanding, and **critical thinking**. Through workshops, seminars, and educational programs, participants can explore the complexities of how historical practices, like slave patrols, have shaped current social structures and biases.

Creating awareness is a fundamental step in initiating conversations and actions to address systemic racism. These initiatives provide platforms for **marginalized voices** to be heard, experiences to be shared, and perspectives to be understood. By **shedding light** on the **deep-rooted issues** stemming from historical injustices, education and awareness initiatives empower individuals to recognize their own biases, privilege, and role in perpetuating systemic racism.

Ultimately, education and awareness serve as catalysts for change, encouraging individuals to become **active allies**, advocates, and agents of anti-racism. These initiatives cultivate a more informed and conscientious society, committed to dismantling systemic racism and fostering equality and justice for all.

Policy Reforms and Advocacy

Understanding the historical context of **systemic racism**, particularly its ties to oppressive structures like slave patrols, illuminates the necessity for **policy reforms** and **advocacy** in dismantling entrenched inequalities. Policy reforms play an important role in addressing systemic racism by reshaping laws and regulations that perpetuate **discriminatory practices**. Advocacy, on the other hand, involves actively campaigning for change by raising awareness, mobilizing communities, and pushing for **legislative adjustments**.

Policy reforms can encompass a wide range of initiatives, such as implementing anti-racism training for law enforcement officers, establishing **oversight committees** to monitor racial bias in policing, and revising sentencing guidelines to reduce disparities in the criminal justice system. Advocacy efforts are equally vital, as they amplify **marginalized voices**, challenge discriminatory policies, and hold institutions accountable for their actions.

Community Engagement and Solidarity

Community solidarity is a foundational pillar in the collective effort to combat **systemic racism** rooted in **historical injustices** like slave patrols. Building solidarity within communities involves fostering relationships, understanding different perspectives, and working together towards a common goal of dismantling racist structures. It requires active engagement, empathy, and a commitment to listening to **marginalized voices**.

One way to promote **community engagement** is through hosting dialogues and forums that encourage **open conversations** about race, privilege, and discrimination. These spaces provide an opportunity for individuals to share their experiences, learn from one another, and collectively brainstorm **actionable solutions**. Additionally, organizing community events, workshops, or **educational programs** can help raise awareness and promote solidarity among diverse groups.

Solidarity also involves standing up against injustice and supporting those who are most affected by racism. This can be achieved through allyship, advocacy, and amplifying marginalized voices. By coming together as a community, we can create a more **inclusive and equitable society** for all.

Conclusion

To sum up, the legacy of slave patrols continues to impact communities today through **systemic racism**. By acknowledging these historical roots, implementing **education initiatives**, advocating for **policy reforms**, and fostering **community engagement**, progress can be made towards addressing these deep-seated issues.

For instance, the city of Richmond, Virginia recently established a Truth and Reconciliation Commission to investigate and address the lasting effects of slavery and segregation on the community. This proactive approach sets a precedent for other cities to follow in seeking justice and reconciliation.

CHAPTER 9: CONCLUSION

Reflection on the Enduring Impact of Slave Patrols

Slave patrols, originating in the 18th century, enforced slave codes and upheld **white supremacy**, influencing **systemic racism** today. Their evolution into structured groups perpetuated inequalities through **racial profiling** and disparities in areas like education and law enforcement. These practices echo in modern injustices, requiring policy reforms and community empowerment to combat. Understanding their historical significance is paramount to dismantling **institutionalized racism** and promoting inclusivity within societal structures. The impact of **slave patrols** continues to shape societal divisions and necessitates a multifaceted approach towards addressing systemic barriers and promoting equity.

Key Takeaways

- Slave patrols' legacy perpetuates systemic racism and oppression.
- Modern adaptations include racial profiling and disparities in healthcare.
- Historical injustices contribute to structural inequalities and discrimination.
- Dismantling their impact requires addressing systemic barriers and biases.
- Promoting inclusivity and accountability in institutions counteracts their enduring influence.

Systemic Racism and Oppression

Investigating the roots of societal structures and historical legacies leads to a profound understanding of the entrenched nature of **systemic racism** and **oppression**. Systemic racism and oppression refer to the **institutional patterns** and practices that systematically disadvantage certain groups based on race or ethnicity. These systems are deeply ingrained in various aspects of society, including education, healthcare, employment, and criminal justice.

In the context of systemic racism, individuals from **marginalized racial or ethnic groups** often face barriers to opportunities and resources that are readily available to others. For example, **discriminatory hiring practices**, **racial profiling**, and **disparities in access** to **quality healthcare** are all manifestations of systemic racism.

Oppression, on the other hand, involves the prolonged cruel or unjust treatment or control over individuals or groups. This can take the form of social, economic, or political marginalization, limiting the agency and autonomy of those affected.

Understanding systemic racism and oppression requires a critical examination of historical contexts, power structures, and **implicit biases** that perpetuate these inequalities. Addressing these issues necessitates collective action, policy changes, and a commitment to dismantling discriminatory systems.

Contemporary Implications and Adaptations

As we examine the current landscape of societal structures and policies, it becomes evident that the enduring legacy of **systemic racism** and oppression continues to shape contemporary realities for **marginalized communities**. The adaptations of historical practices like slave patrols are still visible today in various forms, such as **racial profiling** by law enforcement, **discriminatory housing policies**, and **disparities in access** to quality education and healthcare.

Contemporary implications of these adaptations can be seen in the **disproportionate rates of incarceration** among Black and Brown individuals, the prevalence of **police brutality cases** targeting people of color, and the persistent **wealth gap** between racial groups. Additionally, systemic racism manifests in subtle ways, such as microaggressions in professional settings, barriers to career advancement for minorities, and **environmental racism** that exposes marginalized communities to health hazards.

Addressing these contemporary implications requires a multifaceted approach that includes policy reforms, community empowerment initiatives, and widespread education on the historical roots of systemic racism. By acknowledging and actively working to dismantle these adaptations of past oppressive systems, society can move towards a more equitable and just future for all its members.

Perpetuation of Inequality

Amidst the intricate web of **societal structures** and policies, the **perpetuation of inequality** remains a persistent challenge that demands critical examination and proactive intervention. The **legacy of slave patrols**, with their roots in maintaining control and enforcing the subjugation of marginalized communities, continues to influence contemporary society. The **systemic biases** embedded within these patrols have evolved into modern-day forms of discrimination, disproportionately affecting communities of color. From **racial profiling** by law enforcement to **disparities in access** to education, healthcare, and economic opportunities, the echoes of **historical oppression** reverberate through present-day social systems.

Structural inequalities perpetuated by the remnants of slave patrols manifest in various facets of life, reinforcing divisions and limiting the prospects of marginalized groups. The interplay of historical injustices, implicit biases, and **institutionalized discrimination** contributes to a cycle of inequality that is deeply entrenched within society. Addressing these disparities requires a multifaceted approach that acknowledges the historical context while actively working towards **dismantling systemic barriers** to equality. By recognizing and challenging the enduring impact of slave patrols on contemporary inequality, society can work towards a more just and equitable future.

Pathways to Dismantling Their Legacy

Exploring strategies for dismantling the enduring legacy of **slave patrols** requires a thorough examination of historical contexts, **structural impediments**, and **proactive interventions** in contemporary societal systems.

To begin, acknowledging the historical roots and functions of slave patrols is essential in understanding their **lasting impact** on societal structures and attitudes towards race. By recognizing how these patrols were used to enforce oppression and maintain power imbalances, efforts can be directed towards unraveling their influence on present-day systems.

Addressing structural impediments involves dismantling **institutionalized racism** and biases that have been perpetuated over generations. This includes reforming policies, laws, and practices that disproportionately affect marginalized communities and **perpetuate inequality**. By actively challenging and restructuring these systems, progress towards equity and justice can be made.

Furthermore, implementing proactive interventions such as **community-based programs**, **education initiatives**, and advocacy for **police reform** can help counteract the legacy of slave patrols. By promoting inclusivity, diversity, and accountability within societal institutions, strides can be taken towards dismantling the enduring impact of slave patrols and fostering a more just and equitable society.

Conclusion

To sum up, the enduring impact of slave patrols remains evident in the **systemic racism** and oppression that persists in society today.

By understanding the historical origins and **contemporary implications** of these patrols, we can begin to **dismantle their legacy** and work towards a more equitable future.

Like a tangled web, the influence of slave patrols weaves its way through our society, but with dedication and awareness, we can unravel its grip on our collective conscience.

BOOKS BY THIS AUTHOR

Hidden In Plain Sight: The Legacy Of Slavery

ASIN : B0C87F9GV7

As young people coming of age in the 21st century, we've all heard about 'the talk' that our parents have with us. But for Black kids, there's a different kind of talk: one where we're taught to be aware of our surroundings at all times and how to protect ourselves from potential danger.
This book is a collection of easily verifiable topics of conversation. I am neither a scholar nor a historian, so I strongly recommend that you and your children do your own research; only then will they truly understand the rules of engagement.

Ai, Race, And Discrimination: Confronting Racial Bias In Artificial Intelligence

ASIN : B0CHCP31ND

From biased hiring processes to skewed criminal justice systems, the impact of AI-driven discrimination is far-reaching and profoundly damaging
As artificial intelligence becomes an integral part of our lives, its inherent biases are proving to be more insidious than anticipated, magnifying the very inequalities it was meant to address.

The First Black Trillionaire: How Black Kids Master Artificial Intelligence

ASIN : B0CGYY82KL

Teaching artificial intelligence (AI) to young Black children holds significant importance, as it has the potential to cultivate fairness in access, empower with technology, and create pathways to future careers.
By integrating AI education early on, Black children can acquire the essential skills and insights needed to navigate the digital landscape actively. This empowers them to engage meaningfully with the technological progress that is reshaping our society.

I Hate My Job: A Journal For Documenting Workplace Discrimination And Harassment

ASIN : B0CDNPT4T7

Employees have the right to work in an environment free from discrimination and harassment, and employers have a responsibility to prevent and address this behavior in the workplace.